NIKKI HAYES

CRYING INTO THE SAUCEPAN

MERCIER PRESS
Cork
www.mercierpress.ie

ISBN: 978 1 78117 499 9

10 9 8 7 6 5 4 3 2 1

A CIP record for this title is available from the British Library

Printed and bound in the EU.

I DEDICATE THIS TO FARAH, MY BEAUTIFUL GIRL.
I SPEAK OUT SO YOU NEVER HAVE TO BE SILENCED.

CONTENTS

PROLOGUE

I was born Eimear O'Keeffe on 7 May 1979. When I was fifteen I was broadcasting for a pirate radio station and, as we were broadcasting illegally, many of us took stage names. I chose the name 'Nikki', adding the 'Hayes' later. I've now been Nikki for longer than I was Eimear and am known to more people by my stage name than my birth name.

I have lived most of my life with Borderline Personality Disorder (BPD), an illness that went undiagnosed until 2015. BPD – which is also known as Emotionally Unstable Personality Disorder (EUPD) – is a serious mental disorder marked by a pattern of on-going instability in mood, behaviour, self-image and functioning. These experiences often result in impulsive actions and lead to unstable relationships. BPD is the most prevalent personality disorder and is associated with severe functional impairment and high rates of mortality by suicide.

I should have been diagnosed the first time I came in contact with the mental health services, when, aged fifteen, I had anorexia. If not then, my condition should have been recognised after an attempted suicide in 1997; and if not then, after my post-natal depression in 2014. Each time I was given a different diagnosis, none fully explaining my symptoms or actions. With each diagnosis I became more confused and convinced there was nothing fundamentally wrong with me. It is likely that my illness went undetected for so long because a lot of how I was feeling and acting was easily explained away by lumping my symptoms under the umbrella term of 'depression', or, as when I was younger, by simply attributing it to attention seeking or just being a little out of control.

I have been blogging for a while now about my struggles, and the feedback that I have been getting from others suffering in silence from mental health issues is what propels me on. I have realised that I can't sit back and enjoy the perks of being in the media while ignoring the fact that I have a podium that I can use to fight for better mental health services in this country, as well as to get people talking. If we don't slay the stigma surrounding mental health before I take my last breath, at least I can go down knowing I did all that I could to raise awareness and keep the conversation going. It is because of this that I felt compelled to write my story. I hope it will help raise awareness of BPD and provide more insight into the condition for both sufferers and the people in their lives. Seeing inside the mind of the sufferer, I believe, will help save lives in the future.

I have met so many inspirational people through social media who are using their voices for change. If I started naming names I know I'd leave as many out as I mentioned, so this is a general thank you to you all, because the only reason our voices are being heard is because we are now shouting together and we will not be silenced – not this time!

AUTHOR'S NOTE:

I have changed certain names in this book to protect privacy. The stories I have to tell are more important than the names of the people involved. Also please be aware that there are some descriptions of self-harm and attempted suicide in the book that some readers may find distressing.

1

LOST IN THE CITY

Hood up, head down – lost in a sea of faceless faces. I've never felt so alone.

Nikki Hayes

I wrote the above line in 2015, not long before I was hospitalised for an acute mental breakdown. I wrote it in a tweet and sent it out into the public domain. When I think back to that moment, I see that I was in severe mental pain as I walked along Dublin's O'Connell Street. The street was full of tourists, workers on their lunch break and school kids clearly bunking off their day of learning. I was in a crowded area and I felt everyone was looking at me, judging me. I imagined them saying the things I already thought about myself:

'She's a bad mother.'

'She's an awful wife.'

'She has scars all over herself.'

'She's a psycho.'

I was seriously ill and I didn't even know it.

Since I've started to speak out about my illness I have been contacted by partners and family members of people who have been diagnosed with BPD. Their first concern is being able to effectively communicate with and support the person they love; secondly, they worry about the safety of their loved ones and the situations they seem to be driven into by their unstable mental state.

But there is hope. People with BPD can live perfectly functional lives. The hardest part is getting the diagnosis because the symptoms of the disorder are so diverse. However, once the diagnosis is made, a treatment plan can be agreed and they can learn to work with it.

I have lost a decade of my life to BPD. I spent that time feeling unworthy, unreasonable, upset and despairing, and suffering from a chronic neediness and illogical thinking. It's frightening to think of some of the situations I managed to get myself into. When it comes down to it, I should be dead. I should have died a long time ago.

A lot of people have asked me about the mood swings I suffer from. They wonder how someone can go from crying, curled up in a ball, to standing on a dance floor doing their best Lady Gaga impersonation within a few hours. The truth is, the mind of a BPD sufferer moves so quickly that everything is frantic. A thought pops into your head and you just do it. If you are feeling very low and someone suggests something fun, you jump on it. Packing your bags and heading to the airport on a whim, for example, may seem carefree and fun, but it's those impulsive decisions that can make someone with BPD endanger themselves.

I remember sitting in a psychiatric ward after a minor

breakdown in 2008, a year after my dad's death. As I spoke to the other patients, I decided in a split second that I didn't need to be there. I was a voluntary inpatient (I had agreed to treatment and wasn't sectioned), so I was free to walk out whenever I wanted. That evening I packed my case and walked free. I got a taxi to the airport and flew to London. The decision-making took two seconds; the journey, including transfers, took two hours. I found myself in the hub of London, Oxford Circus. I remember thinking – *how can I be ill?* I went to dinner in the exclusive L'Atelier restaurant, a bottle of wine my perfect companion. I spotted Hollywood actress Julianne Moore at the table next to me. My mood darkened as I drank the entirety of my perfect companion (the bottle of wine and my solitude weren't a good combination). After the meal, I retreated back to my hotel and made my way to the roof with every intention of jumping off. A phone call to my sister was all that talked me down.

Another time I spontaneously agreed to jump out of a plane for charity. The lead-up to the skydiving involved a broadcast from the Galway Races, the day spent in the Fianna Fáil tent, drinking copiously. Then I went on to the g Hotel to judge a best-dressed lady competition before I fell into bed quite intoxicated around 2 a.m. The next morning I woke, hit the road for Birr in Co. Offaly and participated in the world record-breaking skydiving attempt with Skydive4Charity. I never thought things through; I just agreed and did it. Nothing about this sequence of events seemed extreme or abnormal to me. I thought nothing about driving so far or doing the skydive after such a late night. I was asked so I did it. And I've always been bad at time management, so quite often I'd be running from one event to another.

A lot of the extreme situations that I found myself in with BPD were most definitely fuelled by the presence of alcohol. I am not an alcoholic, as I don't crave alcohol, but when I am being extreme and reckless it is mostly alcohol standing there lighting the fire. Because of the high levels of medication I am on, I have made the decision not to drink any more, as I cannot treat it with respect and I haven't reached a stage where I can control myself if drink comes into play. It has been with the help of my medical team that I have learned to admit that it is a crutch when the going gets tough and a crutch that leads to erratic moods and thoughts, and potentially embarrassing situations.

One example of this was when I was invited to London by Microsoft to launch their new computer console, the Xbox 360. It was a swanky affair in the Embankment area of London. The party was attended by celebs such as Calum Best, members of the cast of *EastEnders* and *Coronation Street*, and the boy band Blue. Inside my mind I felt like a fraud. Someone like me didn't belong with all these celebrities. However, on the outside I introduced myself to everyone, while drinking cocktails all night to the point where the actor Philip Olivier shouted at me: 'Any more sea breezes, Irish [my name for the evening], and you'll be floating back home tomorrow.'

I was thrilled. I was being accepted by people that I watched on television. I had my photo taken with the actor

Will Mellor, Duncan from Blue and Martin from *EastEnders*. I didn't even know his real name, so for the night I addressed him as Martin. I don't remember getting back to my hotel, the swish St Martin's Lane.

An alarm woke me at 6 a.m. It was an early flight back. I met the PR team and we groggily made our way to the airport. We ended up on a blustery flight home. Winds were high and the ride was bumpy. My stomach was still feeling delicate from the night before. I remember standing up at one point to make my way to the toilet. I was going to be sick, I was certain of it. I looked ahead. There was Ronan Keating, sitting ahead of me.

'Hi Ronan.'

Then Blcceuuuggghhhhhh.

Oh my God, I just puked in front of Ronan Keating.

Ronan looked pityingly at Nicola, the PR girl who had been sitting beside me on the plane. She ushered me to the bathroom as Ronan did a little laugh to brush off the scene I was making. I stayed in the bathroom for a while, puking, and then emerged, ghostly white. I looked to Ronan to mouth 'Sorry' and he just smiled.

I turned crimson and pulled up the hood on my jumper. I died a death for the remainder of the journey home in more than one way.

The industry I work in lends itself to the lifestyle I had adopted. It is seen as being somewhat normal or acceptable to combine alcohol and socialising in your day-to-day work. There is always a product launch, a venue opening, always a reason to pop the cork and share some bubbly. I lived, ate and slept my job. I was always turning up in the social pages of the newspapers and entertainment websites. I would turn up to the opening of an envelope and, with free food and drink, it didn't cost me a penny – just my dignity. I would mingle, make connections, shoot the breeze and exchange numbers. I felt accepted when I was Nikki. People liked Nikki and they liked what she brought to the table.

Today, acquaintances and people I've worked with over the years find it funny, at first, when I say that I don't drink any more.

'Haha, good one.'

Then they realise from the expression on my face that I'm serious.

'Oh, fair play to ya. Do you not miss it?'

The weird thing about my not drinking now is how it unsettles others more than me. My friends have always known me to be wild and unpredictable. Workmates have always known me to be a bit mad and uncontrollable. My family have always known me as dramatic and needy. So standing in front of everyone, sober, means they don't quite know how to receive me. I find I am approached with caution. Is this a trick? Are they being lured into a false sense of security? Maybe this is the moment she blows up.

A ticking time bomb is not what I set out to be, but it's how I am viewed by my nearest and dearest, and most definitely by my peers. For them, they learned to live with the mood bursts. It didn't mean that they were okay with how I behaved, it just became normal, and I suppose the only way they could somewhat normalise my behaviour was to say that I was unpredictable and wild. By doing so, they could then apply a certain label to me. Everyone has a place in society, a box in which to fit, and for me the box was to be 'mad' or 'wild'. If it meant people could accept me, then it was a label that I was happy to take. Acceptance was all that mattered to me.

The major issue with accepting the label I had been given, however, was that it meant I fell further into the bracket of the unknown. I was being this person because it meant they could accept and make sense of me, but by being this person I felt out of control. If you keep taking on all the traits and personalities that others expect you to have, you very quickly suppress who you are deep down, the core you. But I felt that the core me wasn't someone people were prepared to know or accept easily, so I adopted different personality traits depending on whose company I was in.

This need for acceptance started at a very young age for me. I remember, when I was five or six years old, running to the shops for the neighbours because I wanted them to like me. Every evening at 6 p.m. I would call and ask for their shopping list and then go to fetch newspapers, crisps, milk – whatever they needed. As I got older, I began to develop different personalities to use with different people so they would accept me – the shy, loving, needy girl; the tomboy climbing trees with the boys – and the more I grew up, the more personalities I created. Adopting each different personality was like putting on a mask. I felt like I was always backstage, lifting the masks and placing them on my stage persona depending on where

I was and who I was with. That visualisation made sense to me. The masks made the personalities seem normal, like I was acting as whoever I needed to be in order to gain acceptance.

Waking every morning with the sadness of not knowing or liking the person you are is upsetting. You have two choices. Pretend and survive, or admit and fail. So I pretended to be someone else and survived for as long as my mental stability could support that choice.

2

IDENTIFYING THE SIGNS

I don't want to see anyone. I lie in the bedroom with the curtains drawn and nothingness washing over me like a sluggish wave. Whatever is happening to me is my own fault. I have done something wrong, something so huge I can't even see it, something that's drowning me. I am inadequate and stupid, without worth. I might as well be dead.

Margaret Atwood, *Cat's Eye*

How do you spot the signs of someone with a personality disorder? I've lost count of the amount of times I've been asked this. But BPD is such a complex diagnosis because there are so many different screaming signs and as many again that go unnoticed. I can only refer to my illness and my experiences.

When I look back I see how dangerous my state of mind was. It's not normal to be at 100 per cent at 9 a.m. and be five per cent by 6 p.m. It's not normal to decide that you are going to jump out of a plane with a hangover. It's not normal to carelessly rally around country roads letting adrenaline lead the way, with safety becoming a distant thought. It's not normal to lose two stone in three weeks and then put it back on in as many. It's not normal to isolate yourself from everyone to the point where you speak to no one in work and come home to your dogs with the only 'human' conversation being the one deep inside your mind.

I lived on adrenaline and never saw the consequences of my actions. I never saw the people that I hurt, the people whose friendships I drove away because I couldn't commit to them.

When I was undiagnosed I never believed that the way I was living my life was wrong – I believed that everything I did made sense. This is because I was only engaging my emotions and was unable to activate my logic. If someone challenged me on my behaviour, I would get defensive and would think that they had the problem, not me.

What's wrong with me?

Nothing, don't be such a bore.

When you have BPD you have a full blindfold on when looking in the mirror. You are always deflecting the attention off yourself and back onto others. When someone questions your disproportionate reactions you become confrontational and say things like, 'Why are you turning on me?' or 'Why are you attacking me?' As well as being defensive, I would take the criticism to heart and become upset. If someone shouted at me, I'd cry. If someone raised their voice even slightly I'd curl into a ball and hug myself tightly, building up a defensive wall.

Another trait of BPD is that you can feel as if someone is talking about you when they're not and convert this paranoid feeling immediately into action – meaning you then treat that person as if they really did say something, forgetting you have no proof, only your gut feeling. 'I know that you said bad things about me so why don't you just admit it!' You justify the manic thoughts and mood swings by telling yourself that it is only a matter of time before this person hurts you and lets you down, anyway, so at least now they know that you are on to them.

It is hard to maintain relationships when suffering from BPD because you truly believe that it's only a matter of time before you are abandoned, so you perversely convince yourself to take the control back and cut the person off before they get the opportunity to abandon you and leave you in a mess. As I was always either extremely happy or extremely sad, it meant that I either loved someone or hated them. There never was a middle ground, and this meant that I missed out on a lot of good people becoming part of my life.

I also hated letting people down. As a result I agreed to do things because it would make other people happy. If I heard someone say 'I missed the bus, I'll be home late now', for example, I would immediately offer to drive them home. Even if it was out of my way, I'd lie and tell them I was going that way. Why would I put myself out like that? It was because I was convinced that by doing so they would like me and accept me. This uncontrollable need to be accepted drove me on. Also, if I could do things for others, then I saw myself in a slightly better light. To have that relief, no matter how short-lived, was a true weight off my mind. The negative voices in my head quietened, my heartbeat slowed and my fear of the world melted away. If I felt that someone wasn't accepting me, however, then it would literally seem like the end of the world.

With medication and treatment I have learned that not everyone in life will like you and you can't control that. It's still a hard one to manage, though. I don't expect anyone to understand this fully. I'm still learning. Again, logic doesn't always apply to my way of thinking. I'm still finding better coping mechanisms and trying to silence the irrational foghorn in my head. I'm still coming to terms with issues, many of which I've struggled with since my childhood.

3

BEGINNINGS

Perfection is not attainable,
But if we chase perfection, we can catch excellence.

Vince Lombardi

Growing up, I often found myself unsure of my feelings and thoughts. If a thought came into my head I often acted on it before I had time to process it. I also had disproportionate reactions to situations. I now know, with hindsight, that the disproportionate reactions and extreme emotions I often felt were the early signs of BPD. At the time, however, I had no explanations for my behaviour.

When I was young, my parents would have the whole family kneel in front of the crucifix at 6 p.m. every evening to say the rosary. I despised the fact that we had to kneel and repeat prayers, particularly when I knew that my friends would be in their houses having dinner and catching up on *Home and Away* or *Neighbours*.

After the rosary we would have our tea and be allowed out to play for an hour before bed. My friends would be chatting about the latest developments in the Australian soaps and I hated that I couldn't join in. One evening, when I was eleven, the girls were crushing on Craig in *Neighbours*, saying how great he was. I didn't want to be left out so I bluffed, talking about him as if I knew all about him and what was going on. But one of the girls, Johanne, knew my sister and so she knew that my parents didn't allow us to watch that soap. She called me out on my lie. The rest of the gang started laughing and mocking me. I panicked. How could I take the focus off me quickly? Without thinking, I picked up a brick and threw it at Johanne. I remember her eyes staring at me in shock and disbelief. Then chaos ensued. I had split her head open; blood was pouring down her face.

My heart raced – what had I done?

A crowd gathered around Johanne. As her mother came running out, many of them pointed at me. I heard that an ambulance had been called. I slunk away and ran home.

Not surprisingly, I was grounded for a month. My extremely upset parents told me that Johanne would require stitches and was going to be off school for a few days. I remember being frightened by my actions. How had things escalated so quickly? In a split second it had gone from talking about a TV show to my being grounded for throwing a brick at one of the girls on the street. I just couldn't understand what made me snap like that.

Later that evening I crept down the stairs. Grounded or not, I felt like I needed to get out. I climbed over the fence in our back garden into one of the neighbours' gardens. They had a big home heating oil tank down at the bottom of their garden. I squashed myself in behind it and cried until I felt nothing but complete emptiness. I could hear my parents calling my name.

When I eventually returned home I was yelled at and then sent to bed. I felt sick as I ran up the stairs, two at a time. I jumped into bed, fully clothed. I was distraught with how the evening had unfolded. As I lay exhausted on the bottom bunk, it was only then that I was able to properly process what I had done and realise how serious it was. The violence of my reaction petrified me and I felt I needed to punish myself. I thought that if I hurt myself maybe it would make everyone else happier.

Given that we lived in a three-bedroom house, it meant that my only brother got his own room and my three sisters and I had to share one room between us. To fit us all in, two sets of bunk beds were squashed into a modest space. That night I put my hands under the slats of the bunk above me. I trapped them there until they went blue and numb. When I released them I got my first 'high' from pain that I had inflicted on myself. I convinced myself that if I made people angry, I could turn that anger back on myself, make myself suffer, and then all would be okay with the world again. But it would be my little secret, nobody needed to know. I truly believed this.

These disproportionate reactions continued throughout my childhood. I remember another incident when I was ten or eleven and playing with two of my sisters in our room. We were playing school. My older sister was the teacher and another of my sisters and I were the students. When I received detention in the game, 'teacher' ordered me to write fifty lines. I started and gave up after around twelve. My sister chastised me and then slapped me with a belt from her wardrobe.

I squealed with fright and pain. I started to cry and my father called up to see what was going on. I screamed at him, telling him what had happened. He called my sisters downstairs. In an instant I picked up the belt again. Something flashed in my mind and I lost any sense of reason. I whipped myself until my skin was stinging. The sharp pain gave me relief. It released the frustration building up inside my head and made it all go away, for a moment at least.

When my mother asked me what had happened, seeing the state I was in, I remained silent, knowing that my silence would further implicate my sister. Afterwards, I lay down on my bed and placed my hands in the slats above. I trapped them there until they went numb.

I never once questioned why I felt the need to go to such lengths on a regular basis to harm myself. But I believed that while I was hurting myself, then at least I couldn't be hurting anyone else.

Another example of my over-reaction to situations happened when I was a little older, about thirteen. Friends of mine were from money. Their dad was a very successful businessman. They had nice stuff and went on holiday to Disneyland most summers. I loved being in their home. I loved being around their beautiful things. Their home was like a show house and they had a Betamax player, which meant we could watch movies – believe it or not in the late 1980s that was quite the luxury.

My friend's father had a boat, a cruiser, docked in Howth. I went with them some weekends to help clean the boat and their father would sometimes take us on a short spin from Howth to Lambay Island. It was such an adventure.

Once, when they were heading to Liverpool on the boat, they asked me to go with them. I immediately ran home to ask if I could go. Bar a trip to Donegal on the John McGinley bus to visit my grandparents every summer, I had never been on holiday and had certainly never left Ireland. So I was terribly excited, as it never occurred to me that my parents wouldn't let me go.

I ran through my front door, calling for my mother. She was in the back garden talking to our neighbour, Mrs McDonald, over the fence. I apologised for interrupting, then blurted out my news and request, which was followed by pleading puppy-dog eyes.

'No,' my mother said.

This was a straight out no. There'd been no consideration; it was clear that this was not happening, full stop. I wasn't expecting that and I was devastated with this very concrete response. I really wanted to go, in fact I had convinced myself that I *had* to go.

My mother turned her back on me and resumed talking to Mrs McDonald.

'Please Mammy.'

'I said no.' Again that tone of finality.

I felt a rush of blood in my head and my eyes flashed – I became completely enraged. The words were out before I even thought about what I was saying: 'Fuck you, you fucker.'

My mother's face turned a shade of purple. I had never cursed in front of my parents before and they never used curse words around us. She was clearly mortified that our neighbour had witnessed this outburst. As she turned to her to apologise, I threw a fit. I flung myself on the ground, legs and arms kicking out, and screamed as if I was being burned alive. Mrs McDonald was clearly shocked at how quickly I had gone from calm and smiley to full-on tantrum.

When the tantrum ended I was shaking from head to toe. I felt like my head was about to burst. That feeling left me confused and frightened. I ran into the hallway, climbed under the stairs and curled myself up into a ball, hiding behind the coats.

I sat there for over an hour, sobbing and shaking. What was wrong with me? The tsunami of emotions I felt was overwhelming. I started to wonder if there was something wrong with me, if I was crazy. Maybe everyone would be happier if I just disappeared? I thought about running away, but the idea of being outdoors alone in the dark petrified me. I felt panicked just thinking about it. I can see now that I was having an anxiety and panic attack, but at the time all I knew was that these feelings were stronger than me, that they felt powerful enough to completely possess me.

My father came looking for me when he came home. I had stopped crying by then and I followed him into the TV room. When I sat down, I realised my legs were still shaking uncontrollably. It often happened that I made myself so upset that the emotion manifested itself in physical symptoms like leg spasms, a racing heart or loss of breath. It always took quite some time for my regular breathing to return so I could control my distress.

Any kind of confrontation, no matter how small it was, could also trigger disproportionate emotional distress in me. I remember how, when we lived in Bray, every weekend members of the travelling community would pull up in their van and go door to door in our estate.

'Any old clothes?'

'Money for food?'

'Milk for the baby's bottle?'

Most of the time households would hand over clothes that the kids had outgrown, spare food or milk, things like that. My dad always gave them a pint of milk and sugar for their tea.

One weekend a young girl called to our door. She was about ten or eleven. I peeked through the kitchen door out into the hallway. She had the longest hair I had ever seen and wore sparkly shoes and a ribbon on her head. My mother answered the door.

'Money for the baby?' the girl asked.

'Sorry,' my mother said, closing the door.

It was lashing rain outside. I imagined this girl, with her baby sister or brother, starving. I pleaded with my mother to reconsider and give her some money. Every Friday we got a treat – crisps or chocolate after tea. I told my mother I would go without my treat if we went after the girl and gave her my twenty pence. I grew increasingly upset; I felt somehow responsible for the safety of the girl who had called to our door.

My father came downstairs when he heard me crying. He asked why I was so upset. When I told him about the girl, he told my mother she should have been more sympathetic to her plea for help. He handed me fifty pence and told me to go after her and give it to her. I saw her at the end of our road and ran up to her, chuffed to be handing over money that would help her. She looked at me as I handed her the money and said, 'God bless you, love.'

I turned and ran home to get out of the rain. I felt good, I had helped someone and they liked me.

But when I walked back into the sitting-room I discovered that the atmosphere had soured. My parents had clearly been arguing. They both looked stressed and my siblings were giving me looks of disapproval. It was clear that everyone blamed me – I had caused this. My initial high from helping the girl was replaced with sharp guilt that I had caused my parents to argue.

I ran upstairs, tears stinging my eyes. How did I always manage to mess up?

I slid under my bunk and lay on the floor. I looked at the wooden slats, on which was scrawled in marker some pictures and many words. The most prominent words were:

I HATE ME

It was written in three different colours and shaded into 3D. The words were angry, sad and desperate – and all directed at myself.

Shading objects into 3D shapes was something I liked to do at the time. The appearance of the cubed square with filled-in shading was something that pleased me aesthetically. Many years later, I was told in therapy that drawing a square can represent stability and trust, and it could be suggested that by shading objects over and over again I was enforcing my desire for both of these things.

That day, as I lay under my bed, surrounded by dust and forgotten toys, it gave me some comfort knowing I had this little part of the house that was mine and no one could touch. It was a place where I felt safe. I lay there for about an hour until I was called downstairs for dinner. I didn't really want to eat. Although I did feel a small bit of hunger, I believed that by denying myself food I would be suitably punished for upsetting everyone. So I just pushed the food around my plate, all the time blaming myself for upsetting everyone just to help a complete stranger and wondering why I felt the need to do so.

I sat in the kitchen alone as everyone else went into the sitting-room to watch *Coronation Street.* I quietly called one of our many cats over to the table and fed her the mash and homemade burger. I wouldn't get into trouble as no one saw the cat devouring my dinner; my parents would think I had finally eaten it. When the cat was finished, I walked out into the hallway and out the front door. I just couldn't be around my family right then. The guilt for causing such trouble was too strong and I was so confused. Helping the girl should have made me happy, but the negativity it created at home completely ruined the gesture. The guilt and confusion quickly turned to anger at myself. How did I manage to get it so wrong all of the time?

When I look back now I feel sorry for my younger self. I had little control over my extreme emotional swings and I struggled to make sense of them. I would easily swing from being agitated to being extremely upset in such a short amount of time. I was so confused that I would cry and sob needily, but then I'd often push people away when they tried to help because I feared what they'd think of the real me. It was a sad and lonely place for a young girl to be, and I wouldn't wish it on anyone.

4

OUT OF CONTROL

Maybe we all have darkness inside of us and some of us are better at dealing with it than others.

Jasmine Warga, *My Heart and Other Black Holes*

My mood swings and emotional tantrums meant that I was often viewed as being a difficult child.

'You're a drama queen.' I heard that quite a bit. Others believed I was just an attention seeker and told me so.

But I wasn't a bad child. I was just very confused and frightened at the power of my mind and at the speed at which it swung from euphoria to desperate lows in a way that I couldn't control.

My father seemed to 'get' me, however. Whenever I was uncontrollably upset he would hug me and talk me round. He seemed to have more patience with me than most and we spent a lot of time together. When I was five or six I accompanied him weekly to the social welfare office. He also used to buy me whatever I wanted – sweets, crisps, all the things my more sensible mother said no to. He often took me into Dublin on the old brown Iarnród Éireann trains. Every Christmas we went into the city to see three different Santas. He brought me to all the activities I wanted to try, from ballet and Taekwondo to majorettes and gymnastics. Whenever my parents argued, I would go out with my dad when he went off to cool down.

It was my father I talked to when I reached milestones in my life. When I got my first period, it was him I had the school call. When I had my first boyfriend I told my father about him. He was there for me for all my big life moments as I grew up. I adored him and when I was with him I felt safe and loved, although even then to some extent I was putting on the mask of the loving daughter, playing a part.

That's not to say my father was perfect. He had struggled for many years with alcoholism, although he quit drinking when I was quite small. I sometimes wonder if the fact that he had to battle his own demons helped him to understand and accept that I was fighting my own.

While my problems had started when I was a child, things started to get really out of control as I progressed through my teens. Like most teens my hormones were raging and I had massive highs with massive lows, but everything was made worse by my complete lack of ability to regulate or control my emotions.

I started to develop a pattern of Obsessive-Compulsive Disorder (OCD), although at the time I didn't know that was what it was. I simply felt the need to do certain routines before I slept every evening to avoid a massive disaster from happening. It started with me lying in bed, afraid to sleep. I would stay awake, waiting for my parents to go to bed, which was normally around 11 p.m. Once they were in bed, I would go downstairs. I would then repeat a mantra/prayer twice and go around the entire house, turning off switches and almost blessing the plug sockets with a hand movement that I believed would stop my home from spontaneously combusting.

'Dear God, please protect me, my family and home. Please keep everyone safe and prevent my home from being broken into or going on fire.'

I believed this was an entirely rational routine, as a family had perished in our town shortly before this when their house had burned down. As a result, I had developed an uncontrollable fear of being burned alive. I had also worked out my escape plan in case fire did break out in our house – I'd throw a pillow out the window into the garden before me and then I'd jump from the upper floor of our three-bed terraced house and land on the pillow. I realised that I would probably break or fracture my ankles or legs from this fall, but I took comfort in knowing that I would at least still be alive.

I fell asleep every night filled with anxiety. I felt that the safety of my family and home were my responsibility – if I didn't complete my ritual something bad would happen and then it would be all my fault.

I spent a lot of time stressing myself out with these thoughts, often to the point of driving myself to breaking point. But I never shared how I felt with anyone. My parents, who soon became aware that I was sneaking downstairs every night, simply put my pacing around the house late at night down to some sort of rebellious act. Perhaps they thought that

I was trying to show them that I was now too old to be sent to bed by them. Who knows? When asked about my actions, I would tell them I was downstairs getting water, but I could tell that they didn't believe me.

The house never burned down, of course, but that fact didn't stop the intense guilt and anxiety I felt every day before I completed my night-time routine.

This obsessive side to my nature manifested itself in other ways. When I was fifteen my friend Dawn called me up one evening with an unusual question: 'Do you fancy doing the women's mini marathon with Fiona, Stephanie, me and a few others?'

I wasn't mad into fitness, but there was no way I was going to be left out of what the girls were doing. I already felt like I was a burden at home to my family, so why not take the opportunity to get out and get some exercise, while also getting to spend time with my friends? It seemed like a win-win situation.

The training plan involved us walking from our houses into Bray three nights a week. That easily covered five kilometres. After a few weeks of training, I was really starting to appreciate the fitness and the fact that people were commenting on my weight loss. Week after week we walked, chatted, gossiped and upped the pace.

'Right girls, let's work it up a little, how about a hike up Djouce?' I suggested.

Djouce Mountain would really test our abilities and stamina. But for me that didn't feel like enough; I wanted to push myself further, do more, work harder than everyone else. I thought, *extra weight would mean extra losses.* So I ordered ankle weights and wore them on our climb. But the extra weight put my body under too much strain and even though I was gaining a high from the adrenaline, I ran out of steam. I sat down on a rock, my chest tight.

'What's wrong with you?' Dawn asked.

I took a deep breath, but it didn't matter. I couldn't breathe. My heart rate started going up, I felt stabbing pains in my chest. I lay down on the ground with my hands on my chest, screaming in agony. I was having what felt like a heart attack.

Dawn's mum arrived and took me to St Columcille's Hospital in Loughlinstown. After multiple tests they couldn't find anything fundamentally wrong with me. But I knew what had happened, as it had happened before. I had been experiencing panic attacks for months but always at home, and I would just stay off school until I felt better.

This time it was different, though, as when I was having a medical assessment they noted that my blood pressure, weight and BMI were quite low. The levels weren't low enough to hospitalise me, but they were low enough for them to refer me to a dietician, while the panic attack alerted people to the fact that things weren't all they seemed with me. However, rather than being glad that these problems had been recognised, it was much easier for me to chastise myself for showing the weakness I was trying to hide.

Couldn't even get that right, could you?

Sadly, over the years I fell out with these good friends,

who didn't know about the underlying issues that were causing my panic attacks and found it difficult to cope with how they manifested. But then, back in the mid 1990s, no one really understood these things.

5

TEENAGE TORNADO

Being deeply loved by someone gives you strength, while loving someone deeply gives you courage.

Lao Tzu

Despite the medical assessment after my panic attack on Djouce, we all went on to complete the ten kilometre women's mini marathon in 1995, donating the money we raised to the Marino Clinic in Bray. After this I continued exercising, because I loved the way it made me feel.

However, my new interest in exercise wasn't enough to give me what I perceived to be the perfect body and it was around this time that my relationship with food started to deteriorate. My mother had always been thin, as was my grandmother – they put it down to their lean genes. Unfortunately I seemed to have inherited my father's genes when it came to body shape. Like my aunts, I was hippy and 'vertically challenged'. As my teenage body developed, I started to carry my weight around my middle.

I had always been partial to sweets, chocolate and crisps – so much so that a neighbour once said to me that she didn't know how I still had a tooth left in my head. There were times that I ate so much that I felt too full for dinner and yet I always had room for dessert. If questioned on why I wasn't eating my dinner, I would say I had eaten at a friend's house. This was sometimes true, but more often than not it was a lie. Of course, this didn't help my weight issues. Very soon the sight of my body disgusted me.

My body image wasn't helped by the fact that my friends were either the chubby, funny type of girls or the thin, popular ones. Although I saw myself as fat and flabby, I didn't have the saving grace of being funny. Boys would use me to bring messages to the other girls because they thought I was a bit of a tomboy and they liked me, and because I was goofy-looking none of the other girls saw me as a threat. I was simply someone for the thin girls to use to get to the boys and for the chubby ones to make fun of. I wore clothes that were two-generation hand-me-downs (the joys of having two older sisters). I always felt like I dressed a decade behind my friends. Whenever I went to sleepovers at their houses I would always forget a top so I could borrow one of theirs and feel glam, even if it was for only one day. Their clothes looked to me like something out of *Smash Hits* magazine. In contrast I hated my plump frame and my freckles and frizzy hair.

I always ended up on the sidelines when my friends were playing tennis, basketball, camogie or hockey. Although I enthusiastically joined in with every activity at the start, I never stuck with any of them. For instance, the hockey crew were either hardy or slim and I felt I was neither. I remember being teased by one of them once for being wobbly around the chest – although this was due to the lack of a proper bra, I convinced myself it was because I was fat. I didn't last long after that. I was also accepted onto the basketball team but never played a competitive game. I was just four foot something and clumsy, after all; it was never going to work. Again I left after a while. This became a pattern and it left my parents frustrated with me and my wardrobe full of unused uniforms. Moreover, I perceived these situations as rejections of me as a person and they hit me hard.

I constantly had chatter in my head, a loud, critical voice telling me: 'You're fat. You're clumsy. You're ugly. No one likes you.'

These words went around and around in my head until they became fact and I completely believed them. I remember the feeling I would get when I looked in the mirror – I was repulsed with what looked back at me – I was disgusting.

With my teenage hormones raging, my body changing and the continuing panic attacks and emotional highs and lows, I felt that there was so little I could control. But one thing I could control, I realised, was what I put into my mouth.

So I stopped eating.

I would avoid breakfast and lunch entirely. My mother worked from the time I was young, so she'd always make the next day's dinner the evening before and leave it in a pot for myself and my siblings. When we came in from school we were supposed to heat up our dinner and eat it. Due to the lack of supervision, however, I started to regularly feed my hearty stew or lasagne to the cats and opt for chocolate or cereal instead. This is no reflection on my mother's cooking – it was entirely my choice to control what I ate by opting not for the nutritious food being provided, but instead going for the sugary quick fix which I would usually be craving after a day of no food.

When my dinner was set down in front of me at the weekends I would push the food around the plate, trying to make it look like I had eaten some of it, when in fact I had eaten nothing. In my head I had the control. If my parents were watching then I would force myself to eat some of the food and then excuse myself. I would rush to the bathroom, where I would stick my fingers down my throat and vomit it all back up again. Looking back I can see that this was the start of my eating disorder and yet another sign of the elephant in the room – BPD.

Not surprisingly, I started to lose weight. Then my schoolmates started to tell me how well I looked, remarking on how much weight I'd lost.

'Skinny mini.'

'You look so skinny.'

'Anorexic Annie.'

Their comments and shocked faces propelled me forward. This was exactly what I needed to keep going. I had never been noticed in school; I was the grey girl, always in the background. Now people recognised me, talked to me, acknowledged me. I loved it. It was exhilarating and encouraged me to keep going.

The weight just kept falling off. I was on a high, I wanted to feel like this always. It was at this point that it stopped being about dieting or training for an event – it became a compulsion, a controlled cycle of:

> I hate me = I starve myself = I feel depressed = I hate myself = I feel depressed = I eat a little = I feel guilt = I purge.

This was a pattern that became routine. It was a vicious circle which repeated constantly.

Around this time I also started cutting myself. Despite this escalation in the violence I was inflicting on myself, I still did not question why I felt the need to harm myself. As with not eating and purging, it gave me a sense of control over my body. It also gave me a high like none I had experienced before. I convinced myself that because I was only hurting myself, it would have no impact on anyone else. Just me. Nobody else would care. When I was caught up by this train of thought – self-hatred, seeking appropriate pain for relief – I felt dizzy, like I was having an out-of-body, euphoric experience. I used to imagine a balloon inside my head, blowing up so that it pushed everything else out of my mind, making all my problems just disappear.

Then, one day, when I was still fifteen, I fainted at school. I felt dizzy and suddenly my feet went from under me. When I came round I felt so tired that I just wanted to sleep for days. There was no more steam left, no more fight. I was referred to a psychotherapist by our family doctor, Dr Hawkins, with a view to hospital admittance in St Vincent's to monitor my eating. This scared me. I didn't want to be labelled as someone who couldn't look after themselves. I wanted to be the same as everyone else, not different. I wanted people to like me, spend time with me, even though I felt unworthy of their time and attention.

Eventually it all became too much. I felt my life was spiralling out of control. One night I snapped, went down the stairs to our medicine cabinet and shoved handfuls of Paracetamol and prescription medication into my mouth. As I waited for the tablets to take effect, I realised that while I wanted the pain building up in my mind to go away, I didn't want to die. I started to cry, then scream.

My father came rushing down and found me. But after calling an ambulance, his inability to deal with the situation came to the surface and he screamed in my face, 'That's it, you're going to die before the ambulance comes.'

I remember looking at him through my tear-stained eyes as he waved and said, 'Bye now, you're going to die.'

When I needed him most, when my life was on the line, it seemed like he had turned against me. I didn't understand. I blacked out.

I came around in an ambulance with two men standing over me. 'Can you hear me?' one of them asked. They talked to me, trying to keep me calm. I slipped back into unconsciousness.

I woke later that evening to find my mother and father sitting beside my hospital bed. My mother was crying, her head turned, trying to hide her distress from me.

My father reached out and patted my hand, saying, 'I love you; you gave me a fright. Don't ever do that again.' I could tell that he regretted his earlier reaction – that he'd simply panicked – and was seeking my reassurance that everything would be okay.

I gave it – of course I did.

This was the first time I was hospitalised due to my mental health issues. Because I had attempted suicide, I was kept there for three days so they could monitor me.

I would have a longer stay in St Vincent's Hospital's psychiatric ward a few months after this, when I was admitted to deal with the anorexia from which I was also suffering. I was admitted to the St Camillus Ward, an adult psychiatric ward. It had been explained to me on admittance that I would be around people with various mental health issues, from acute to slight. I was also told that I would be given meals and monitored by nursing staff as well as attending my psychiatrist.

Walking the corridor with the nurse who admitted me, I honestly had no idea what to expect, but I do remember thinking that I would fit in here. Then I passed a young man – no more than twenty years old – who was going into the TV room. That gave me a fright, as he was drooling and his eyes were glazed – it was the first time I had contact with someone who was very mentally ill. I found out later that he had severe psychosis.

I was staying in a three-bed room off the nurses' station. There was one empty bed and the other was occupied by a girl around my age. The nurse checked me in, then took away my shoe laces, my hair dryer and the belt out of my dressing gown. This routine is one I'm now familiar with. Every time you are admitted to a psychiatric ward any items that you could use to harm yourself or another patient are removed. Simple things like charging your phone or straightening your hair become timed events – if you don't finish them swiftly, the nursing staff arrive to check that you're not doing something to self harm.

After I had settled in my room, I pulled back the curtain separating myself and the girl beside me. She was so pretty. Her father was sitting beside her showing her the hurling match that had taken place that week. I got a rush of confidence/ verbal diarrhoea. I wanted her to like me, to accept me. I introduced myself and she politely shook my hand, as did her father, who then excused himself to go get a coffee and 'let you girls get to know each other'. Her name was Thelma and she was from Wexford. She was admitted because she was suffering with bulimia, another eating disorder, so we had something in common.

Later that evening we both ventured up to the television room. I was shocked. Although admitted for anorexia, I felt I looked obese compared to some of the girls sitting watching *Coronation Street*. There was one girl in particular who was literally skin and bone. Her eyes were sunken and sad. She shied away from us, avoiding eye contact so she wouldn't have to talk. She was a severe case – she was being fed from a feeding tube, attached to an IV drip and had a nurse with her full-time. I was shocked that this could be my future if I continued down the road I was on. But the shock swiftly moved to admiration. I was in awe of her strength, her ability to abstain from food. It made me see that I wasn't strong, I was fat. I was in hospital being treated for anorexia but I felt fat.

During my time in Vincent's, I did get to know the girl with the sunken eyes and her, Thelma and I became friendly. We were bound by a common goal – self-destruction.

The days in the hospital were spent attending psychiatrist appointments, weigh-ins and occupational therapy classes – colouring, crafts and creative writing. I found these classes extremely therapeutic. They mostly took place in silence or with strained conversation from the teacher. Most people just didn't want to share; their pain was so raw that talking about it would drop them to their knees in uncontrollable tears. I didn't feel that same desperation; I felt elated when I starved myself.

I talked to the other patients, learning more about eating disorders and picking up all the tricks of the trade. I was educated about laxatives, diuretics and purging. I learned how to deceive those close to me into thinking that I was in control, that I was okay. The extent of my eating disorder was my secret and I could keep it that way. Anorexia for me became a wall to hide behind, my secret control over how my life was unravelling. Anorexia is thrilling: you are inflicting pain on yourself and you feel elated to have this big secret that you can hide from the world. But I now know that with any mental health issue, you can't hide it forever. It eventually catches up with you and exposes you for the fraud you are.

Years later, my sister Caroline showed me a photograph of myself from that period of my life. That photograph frightened me – I was skin and bone. My complexion was pale, my hair was thin at the front and my school uniform hung off my frail shoulders. I looked sick and so fragile, yet I can still remember how I felt at the time. I felt in control, powerful, like I finally fit in. I believed that I could exist on this planet in my new shell and have a good life.

Looking at that photo, however, I also felt a desperate sadness for my younger self – the warning signs all pointed to BPD, yet it would be another twenty-two years before the diagnosis was made.

6

ESCAPING INTO THE WIRELESS

Remember that girl you called fat?
Remember that girl you gave a dirty look to?
Remember that girl you called ugly?
She's dead.

Nikki Hayes

During this troubled time, I would often escape into music and different radio stations. I had, after all, grown up listening to the radio. My father loved music – in the 1960s he ran jazz clubs with his friend Noel. Listening to the radio was something we were raised on.

There was a time when we were children that we didn't have a TV in our house, so the radio was our main source of entertainment. I remember my mother buying a world radio tuner, which meant you'd get the English channels like BBC Radio 1, albeit in awful quality. I loved it – the presenters sounded exotic and the music was better than anything being played on Irish radio at the time. My siblings listened to heavy metal and rock, whereas I was drawn to mellow rock and power ballads.

I spent my teens religiously listening to and calling Tony Fenton's *Hotline* on RTÉ Radio 2. Radio mesmerised me. These people talked to me every day, I heard their voices and enjoyed their humour. At that time in the 1990s a lot of DJs had stage names and – as the rise of social media had yet to happen – they were shrouded in a cloud of mystery.

I never had aspirations to be on radio myself. Given the way I felt about myself, I thought I'd never be good enough. It was only when doing transition year in school that I decided to try to get work experience at a radio station. I applied to East Coast Radio nearby in Bray and DLR FM, a pirate station in Dún Laoghaire. I received a letter back from East Coast saying they had no places left for transition years, but then got a phone call a day later from DLR to say that they'd love to have me. A friend of mine, Julie, fancied seeing the radio station too, so we spent a week together in the shed that housed the station, watching the pros put together and broadcast their radio shows.

I was in awe of the way these voices were brought to life in front of me, the way the microphone opened and the voice that had spoken to me moments before off-air now changed, as if by magic, into something deeper, richer, funnier and more appealing. This transformation made sense to me; it appealed to me. It didn't matter who you were in life, in radio you could be whoever you created as soon as you switched on your microphone to talk. You could even change your name.

As the week came to an end, I knew I didn't want to leave. Neither did Julie. We asked the station manager, John Daly, whether we could stay on at the weekends and help out. John was like a country music star straight from Nashville. He wore cowboy boots with tassels, stood well over six feet in height, and even had a cowboy hat. 'Sure, why not,' he said. 'Actually I have a free slot tomorrow morning if yas fancy presenting it?'

Whoooooaaaaa, this is escalating quickly, I thought. Far too excited to care, we both agreed immediately. Since it was an illegal broadcast I couldn't use my own name, so I became Nikki – just because I liked the sound of the name. I would add the Hayes a few years later, taking it from Colm Hayes on FM104, whose show I listened to. When I got to know him, Louis Walsh used to slag me about being Colm's love child!

Looking back on the show we ended up co-presenting for a few months, we sounded young, giggly and immature. But I had certainly found something that I was passionate about. I adored the secrecy and the ability to be whoever you wanted to be that radio presenting gave you.

My parents weren't delighted with the fact that I was going to a shed in Dún Laoghaire to broadcast illegally every week, but I soon made it clear to them that I was going to do this with or without their consent. It was the first time that I felt I truly belonged somewhere.

7

LEGALLY BLONDE

Depression is like a bruise that never goes away.
A bruise in your mind.
You just got to be careful not to touch it where it hurts.
It's always there, though.

Jeffrey Eugenides, *The Marriage Plot*

In August 1997 it was time for me to leave home – well, Monday to Friday anyway. I was moving to Donegal as a student at Letterkenny Institute of Technology (LIT). I would be doing legal studies, which, as my father pointed out, 'is a great course with great prospects for you. Your cousin Laura did it and look where she is now, working in a bank. And we'll have her to look out for you up there, and your nanny and granda are only an hour away.'

Finally a chance to spread my wings and not be seen as:

'The anorexic.'

'The psycho.'

'The weird one.'

Instead, I had a clean slate.

Being away from home gave me a level of freedom that I

had never experienced before. I was convinced I could create a fantastic persona and everyone would like me, so I decided to make myself the happiest, most positive person I didn't know.

I moved into digs with girls from all over the country and impressed them with the fact that I was a DJ. Although I had been doing pirate radio the last few years, I had never gigged in a nightclub. Still, I told them about the great parties I had performed at and the famous DJs I had worked alongside. Some of the stories were true, but most of them were fabricated. *Sure it's not me I'm talking about anyway*, I thought. *I'm only being who these people want me to be.*

I had been on anti-depressants since my hospital stay for anorexia in 1995 but I stopped taking them when I left for college. With my urge to fit in, and having convinced myself that I was this new, reinvented version of myself, I decided I was okay. I didn't need the medication. I was just like everyone else.

Looking back, I can see that from that point on things went quickly downhill. However, at the time, in my eyes things just seemed to be getting good. I had more friends than I could deal with. It was as if my life was finally falling into place.

After a few months living in digs with strict house rules, I made an impulsive decision: *I'm going to get my own place.*

Big mistake.

I took myself away from the digs my parents had found for me. I managed to convince my parents that a few girls had moved out with me although, truthfully, there were only two of us.

If I think back to that year I can only describe it as 'manic'. I mean, most people go to college and enjoy a vibrant social life, but still manage to balance it with an active study life. But when I look back at my time in college, it's dark and blurry. The social part of my being took control very quickly. The ups and downs were extreme. I can recall images in my head of friends handcuffing me to a bath while the water overflowed and flooded the bathroom; of myself sitting in the kitchen, drinking vodka and peach Schnapps. I felt so happy. My friends loved me and I loved the person I had created for them.

I was fun. I was interesting. I was totally out of control.

8

IMPLOSIONS

When you are surrounded by all these people, it can be lonelier than when you're by yourself. You can be in a huge crowd, but if you don't feel you can trust anyone or talk to anybody, you feel like you're really alone.

Fiona Apple

I wish someone could have saved me from the monster I created. I was on a self-destruct mission, determined to totally erase the old me. I drank day and night. I missed lectures and got a reputation throughout the college for being a wild party person. And I was. I paid for everyone into clubs and paid for their drinks and loaned them money and bought them clothes. I wasn't well off – my parents were working hard to support me – but I was making sure every penny was being invested in the new, better me. The sad part of this is that I wasn't a spoiled brat. I hardly spent a penny on myself. I used the money to buy friends and they came in droves.

I'm not trying to justify any of this, I promise; I just want to try to steer you into my mindset at the time. I truly believed this new me was the person I was always meant to be – she wasn't even me, really; she was the DJ, she was Party Central, she was unstoppable. I convinced myself that I had become someone to be noticed.

The highs I was feeling couldn't last, of course; no one can live unaided at extreme highs.

By January 1998 I had been spending my weekends up in Letterkenny for a while and hadn't been home in two months, except for three days at Christmas. I had fallen out with my parents because I wanted to move to Letterkenny full time and get a job. (I had dropped out of my legal studies course at this point, having fallen behind on the course work, although my parents didn't know this yet.) My parents didn't approve of this plan. 'You can come back here to Bray for the summer and get a job,' they argued.

I knew that if I went home I'd go back to being Eimear – boring, friendless, awkward Eimear. There was no way I was letting go of the new me.

But I was struggling – being away from home, under the influence quite a lot, having people expect things from me, being constantly switched on, playing who I thought people wanted me to be. I was in a very dangerous state of mind. If I went to a local nightclub and was offered acid, I took it. Ecstasy? I took it. Hash brownie? I took it. (I have never smoked, so brownies were the only way I would take hash – well, either that or in a yoghurt.) There were the inevitable downers that followed from these drugs, of course, and that's when friends would provide Valium, sleeping tablets, or whatever else I needed to get me through.

I was also afraid of my own mind; the more I lived this lifestyle the darker my thoughts became. The more I detached from reality, the deeper I slipped into thoughts of self-harm and self-hatred. I started to think about dragging a knife down my arm. I remembered the release I had felt when I'd done this before. Maybe it would make me feel better?

One night, intoxicated, during a party at my house, I swallowed a few months of untaken medication in my bedroom and put my headphones on. The song 'Stay' by Sash! filled my head. I started crying to the point where I was roaring and rocking. I felt out of control; I didn't know who I was. I burst into the party and screamed at everyone: 'Leave me alone! Get out get out get out!'

No one listened. They just kept cheering and chanting my name.

Why won't they listen to me? Why doesn't anyone ever listen to me?

I'd had enough. I went back to my bedroom, pulled the wardrobe across the door so no one could get in and cut my arms until they bled and stung. I started to feel sleepy.

I wanted my mind to leave me alone. I wanted my mum and dad. I wanted to go home. But I couldn't let them know that all this had happened, so instead I simply lay there, drifting in and out of consciousness.

Eventually someone tried to open my door to get me to come out. Seeing the door was blocked one of the guys at the party ran around to my bedroom window and climbed in. He quickly realised that I was not in a good way, what with my body turning grey and blood everywhere, so an ambulance was called. I was brought to the local hospital and given a strong dose of IV fluids to flush the toxins from my system; it was too long from the time I had overdosed for them to use charcoal to bind the drugs and stop them being absorbed until my body could repel them naturally.

One of my friends, Alan, came to see me the following day. A nurse sat near my bed, monitoring me. The minute I saw Alan I felt immense guilt for dropping my mask.

Why can't I be stronger? Why don't I just suck it up and get back to normality?

I had no idea what normal was, of course, swinging from one extreme to the other – not even daily or hourly, but from minute to minute. I decided at that moment, hooked up to machines, that I was leaving the hospital. Sure, I was grand. The nurse tried to hold me, called the doctors, called security but I ran with Alan, who'd believed me when I claimed to be fine, beside me. I don't know how I managed it but I ran and ran and ran until I reached the town. It was a rush, and Alan was delighted with the entertainment that I had provided.

Alan was a good guy, one of many that I met when I was in Letterkenny. That day we went to a local pub. Alan ordered me a drink, but unusually, after one, I really didn't feel great and wanted to go home to bed. I remember Alan walked me to the taxi rank and the next thing I knew I was waking up back in hospital.

My head was bandaged, I quickly realised, and I was attached to a monitor and had a nurse sitting beside me. Had I just imagined the whole running-away scenario? I wanted to ask what had happened but instead fell back to sleep.

I didn't realise at the time that all of this was taking place over a number of days, so my usual check-in with my parents hadn't happened. When I finally realised that almost a week had passed since the house party I panicked and pleaded with the nurse that I be allowed to call home. The nurse grudgingly helped me out to the phone in the corridor only steps from my bed.

'Hello?' my older sister answered formally. We were always told to answer the home phone in a professional manner as my father worked from home as a bookkeeper and accountant.

'Hi, is Daddy there?'

'No, where are you?'

'I'm in Donegal. I've just been busy at college.' Even in this state I had another face on. 'I wasn't going to tell anyone, but–'

My sister cut me off. 'Stop the crap, Eimear. Mum and Dad are on their way up to Donegal. The doctors called and you're in deep shit.'

I hung up and swallowed hard, panic rising in my throat. I still felt quite unstable on my feet, so I held the wall for support. I tried to think back to when I was admitted. I could have sworn I had told the doctor that I didn't have any next of kin. That sounded about right, as I hadn't wanted anyone to know this had happened. I was eighteen, after all, so they couldn't go against my wishes. Or so I thought.

It turns out the doctor wasn't confident I would survive and was worried for my welfare when I had run from the hospital.

They contacted the college, who provided them with my next of kin's details. One true friend had also told their parents, who lived in Letterkenny, and they, in turn, had spoken with my parents. They promised my parents that they'd ensure I didn't leave the hospital again.

But how could I? My head pounded as if a rock had been dropped on it. My skin was grey (an adverse reaction to the overdose I had taken) and my arms were bandaged from the cuts.

It turns out that I had suffered a brain seizure at the taxi rank the day I had run out of the hospital. It caused me to have a fit. Alan was convinced, he told me later, that I was going to die. He called friends of ours from the ambulance, saying he was on the way to the hospital and was pretty certain I was dead.

Yet even after all of this I could only wonder why everyone was fussing. I felt it was a lot of bother about nothing. Why couldn't I just go back to normal?

I was reluctantly released from hospital into the care of my parents.

9

AN APPLE A DAY

Suicide is a permanent solution to a temporary problem.

Robin Williams

At home in Bray the next morning everyone was so awkward around me. My younger sister looked at me pityingly. My parents would barely meet my gaze. I tried to convince them to let me go back to Donegal.

'I'm grand,' I argued. I thought if I could convince my parents that I was all right, then they would forget everything that had happened.

'You are not going back there,' mum said. 'We are having your stuff collected and you're going to America to your sister.'

My eldest sister, Ann-Marie, was living in New York at the time. I was pretty sure she wouldn't be delighted with this decision.

I guess at that point my parents really must have felt that they couldn't control me – shipping me across the Atlantic was their last resort. But I also couldn't control myself. So I decided to just accept what they said. *I can always start again*, I thought.

New me.

Clean slate.

Hellloooooo New York.

10

FORGET THE CITY, I NEVER SLEPT

We must be willing to let go of the life we have planned so as to have the life that is waiting for us.

Joseph Campbell

I was excited. I'd never flown before and now I was off to America on my own. I was going to New York, staying in Manhattan. Ann-Marie was a director at a school there and the owner was taking me on as a classroom assistant at the playschool/nursery as a favour to her. I was getting the opportunity to reinvent the tainted me in a whole new country.

New York was everything I ever could have wished for. I was treated like an adult. I was surrounded by exciting people and places: I walked in Central Park, watched men play chess at Battery Park and took in colour that I had never experienced before on Christopher Street. The cork was popped off New York and, in those first weeks, I couldn't drink enough of it.

However, week by week I found the pressure of the city bearing down on me. It was all go and the days were long. I was up from 7 a.m. working and not home until 8 p.m. My inner demons were banging on the door and I was finding it difficult to keep them at bay.

You're an idiot.

You're ugly, fat, a waste of space.

After a few weeks in New York, I had only one clear thought – and that was of hurting or even destroying myself. I was living the dream in Manhattan and yet all I wanted to do was die. That's how quickly my mood and mind shifted. Despite being in the Big Apple I realised that I didn't want to be on earth at all.

My sister's partner also didn't seem to want me staying with them. They were in a one-bedroom apartment. I heard the whispers from him and the soothing from Ann-Marie. Once I thought I heard him call me 'a slob'. The word slob for me sounded right. I was ugly, fat and useless – 'slob' fitted that perfectly. It also played into my self-hatred, fuelling me to source a knife and punish myself.

Looking back, I wasn't a slob; I was simply a teenager sleeping on a camp bed in the living room of a small apartment. I understand that he couldn't move through his own house without seeing me but I was horribly self-conscious and his apparent rejection confirmed for me the fact that I was worthless.

No one likes you because you're disgusting.

I had put on four pounds during my time in New York – was my weight going to spiral out of control? My biggest fear – of being unable to control my weight – felt real. I needed help. I needed to die. *Maybe dying in New York is the way I'm meant to go?*

I started to write down my anger in journals and I signed up to pro-ana websites, which provide a platform for a community of people who think anorexia and various other eating disorders are fashionable. There were community chat rooms that were used for people to help each other lose weight drastically. I even researched ways to commit suicide.

I had been due to stay in New York until the summer but I realised that would be a bad idea and so I called my parents and told them I wanted to come home. I was hysterical on the phone. My father said that he would try to get me a flight. He called back later that day to tell me that a flight had been arranged for me the following day, 17 March. It seemed the St Patrick's Day night-time flight from JFK to Dublin wasn't the busiest. So it was with tears and hugs and thanks to Ann-Marie that I boarded my Aer Lingus flight home to Dublin.

11

RADIO WAVES

Music lowers the levels of the stress hormone cortisol and renders people less stressed.

Unknown

Once back in Dublin, I returned to radio – the one solid want in my life. Behind the back of the DART station in Bray a few local lads had set up a pirate station – Passion FM. I knew a lot of them as they had previously worked in DLR. I approached the station manager and asked if I could have a show. He agreed and I started presenting, delighted to be back on the airwaves. Radio is a bug and once you catch it you are hooked for life.

One day, about six months after I'd returned, the Office of the Director of Telecommunications Regulation (ODTR) arrived at the station while one of the DJs, Barry O'Neill, was mid-show. He got word out to us and we all raced down to the studio. He had the door barricaded by the time we arrived, but the ODTR had already done what it had set out to do. They had left a Cessation to Broadcast Notice on the door and had confiscated most of the equipment. We were gutted.

The Passion FM team had a great relationship with our listeners in Wicklow and south Dublin. We knew this from their feedback when they turned up to themed events run by the station. On the day we were due to cease broadcasting, we put out a notice for our listeners to join us for one last song. I couldn't believe the amount of people who turned up – the storage yard beneath the studio was packed. We all individually took to the roof of an adjacent prefab and said our own little pieces about how we'd miss the station and the listeners. Rob G, one of my fellow DJs, squeezed my hand and then clapped the listeners as the final song, Honeyz' 'End of the Line', played out on the speakers. There was a huge round of applause, whooping and hollering as the song ended. Then silence. The day the music died.

I knew what I wanted – I had a desperate need to hide behind a microphone and be whomever I desired. After the closure of Passion FM I contacted every radio station I could think of to try to get work experience, but to no avail. Then I came across a job offer for an advertising sales executive with East Coast Radio. I realised that this would be an ideal way for me to get my foot in the door. So, even though I had no experience in sales, I decided to go in and sell my love for radio in the hope that they would see my enthusiasm and take me on.

I can still clearly remember walking into CEO of East Coast Radio Sean Ashmore's office for that interview – nervous but determined. He shook my hand and I sat down. Half an hour later I left with a job. I was shocked and thrilled all at once. I'd start Monday.

12

YOU ASKED FOR IT

You are not your illness. You have an individual story to tell. You have a name, a history, a personality. Staying yourself is part of the battle.

Julian Seifter

By the early 2000s there was a vibe in Irish radio that I had never seen before. Commercial radio was thriving and music was everyone's favourite thing. Stations were buying mobile broadcasting vehicles and international sponsors were running massive promotions across the airwaves.

At this time I was still selling advertising at East Coast FM, but I was also presenting a show at the weekends and helping with street promotions in their promotional jeep. Everything was fitting together nicely and I was happy to be back behind the mic. I was comfortable. I loved being with East Coast. At the same time, I craved the excitement that the Dublin commercial radio scene was offering, like invites to the biggest events and parties.

A new station was coming to the market called SPIN 1038. It would be purely focused on the under-thirty-five age group, and one of the major shareholders was the Ministry of Sound.

There was talk of fresh young talent and plenty of parties and money. The press were really excited about SPIN as it was the first time Ireland would have a proper, edgy youth station. So I thought: *Why not? What do I have to lose?* I sent off a demo and crossed my fingers and toes, everything, hoping that I may be considered for some airtime.

A few weeks passed and, convinced I hadn't made the cut, I tried to curb my disappointment. My father suggested that maybe sales was the area I was meant to work in and that radio could be my sideline option. I started to believe that. Then one day, as I drove to another appointment, my phone lit up.

'Hello?'

'Hi, it's Liam Thompson here from SPIN 1038. Can you talk?'

My heart stopped. 'YES.'

'We received your demo tape and CV and would love to see you for interview.'

Stay calm, stay calm, stay calm.

'Yes, that would be great.'

'How's tomorrow at ten o'clock?'

My roots are in bits. I need to get an outfit. Panic panic panic.

'Perfect, I look forward to it.'

I ran around that afternoon and evening, getting my hair coloured and raiding my wardrobe and my sisters' wardrobes to find something suitable to wear for the interview. I was pumped and scared at the same time. I wanted it so badly. I needed to get it or I knew I'd be devastated.

Straight after the interview the following day, I felt confident that I had asked the right questions and answered the way they wanted me to. But as the day progressed I began doubting myself. I wouldn't get the job. I wasn't the right person. I wasn't good enough.

My phone rang at 8 p.m.

'Hey, it's Liam Thompson here from SPIN.'

I held my breath.

'We'd love to offer you the position of full-time presenter of the shift.'

I squealed. I didn't need to think about it at all.

'YES! YES! YES!'

The shift I was being given was a night-time show that played R&B and chilled music. It was five days a week. This was going to be a proper job, a proper job in radio. I felt like I'd won the lotto.

I heard Liam laugh and he said he'd send out the contract and make arrangements for me to come in and meet the team. In that moment I seriously felt like the world was mine and, finally, I had found a little piece of me that I actually liked.

13

MOULDING NIKKI

I'm not the kind of girl you can easily understand.

Nikki Hayes

I began to build my work persona from the day I started on SPIN 1038. The station was so fresh and young that no one knew each other and the opportunity was available to be whoever you wanted to be. I wanted to be wild, I wanted to be fun, I wanted to embrace city life. SPIN 1038 was a new, exciting brand and we were all caught up in the magic of being labelled the next big things in radio.

It was thrilling. Working in the city led to a lot of events and parties and, being the new kids in town, everyone wanted us on their guest list. This was the world I had dreamed of, the one that let you be whatever you needed to be and didn't judge. My show was gaining interest and I was throwing myself out into the social scene, going to Dublin's top nightspots, being treated to free entry, free drinks and plenty of excitement. I was hooked.

In this environment I didn't have to be mentally ill Eimear, the girl who had been diagnosed with anorexia and battled depression. Now I was a recognised DJ, Nikki Hayes, and I was going to live my life to the full.

Things happened very quickly for me, career-wise, around this time. After a year and a half on SPIN 1038 I got a call from the national broadcaster, RTÉ 2FM. This was September 2003. I had grown up listening to this station, which was the pinnacle of Irish music broadcasting. This is where you aimed for as an Irish DJ. They didn't have a full-time position but wondered if I would be interested in eight weeks of work covering for one of their established presenters.

Again, I didn't even stop to think. 'Yes!'

Afterwards I thought – *Oh, will I lose my job on SPIN if I do this?* Thankfully it turned out that John Clarke, the then programme director at 2FM, had already asked Liam Thompson for permission to contact me. Liam had been the assistant programme director at 2FM before he took over the role of programme director at SPIN 1038. They were long-time colleagues and friends, and had agreed that this was a great opportunity for me and I could do the eight weeks on a Sunday with 2FM while still doing my five-day week on SPIN 1038. In the end this eight weeks turned into a full-time position on 2FM.

Looking back, I think I didn't have strong enough personal support networks in place as my career propelled forward. It all happened so fast – too fast, maybe. I was putting a massive amount of pressure on myself to succeed and when I was offered the job on 2FM I vowed never to give less than 110 per cent. The general reaction to this new opportunity only spurred me on. My grandfather, Hubert, a former Royal Air Force man who didn't believe in showing emotions and had never really acknowledged my career choice, was suddenly telling everyone who'd listen that I was his granddaughter. My father couldn't have been prouder; even critics within the radio industry seemed to warm to me. I felt as if the world was mine for the taking.

14

SMILING AMONGST THE STARS

I live in a vicious circle of self-hatred.
I create it and it consumes me.

Nikki Hayes

When I was at the start of my career in RTÉ, I made friends with the people who were always on a guest list. One person in particular, Niall McCrudden, befriended me and took me under his wing. He was a gentleman with a very big heart. He made me feel like one of the important movers and shakers in the city. Thanks to him I went to the best parties and met the people I had always idolised from afar. He introduced me to people I never would have met otherwise.

Niall was the nicest guy you could meet; he always had a smile and a brand new suntan. He owned a chain of opticians and a sunglasses business and, as one of the main men on Dublin's social scene, he was loved by all. I remember him inviting me to a party he was throwing with Keith Duffy in the Clarion Hotel on the quays. It was the night of Skyfest, a festival run by 98FM. Dublin's skyline above the Liffey was lit up and we had a prime position out on the balcony in the penthouse. My friend Audrey had come with me, and we were star-struck by a lot of the big names who were present.

I first met Audrey when I returned from New York in 1998. We had both been attending a DJ course, learning how to beatmix tunes together for nightclub work. Audrey and I connected immediately; she was a tomboy and a laugh. She was always cracking jokes and made me feel at ease, as if I didn't have to try to impress her. So when Niall said to bring a friend, it was always going to be Audrey that I brought.

It was at that party that I first met Ray Shah, after his stint on the reality show *Big Brother*. I met models, TV stars like George McMahon and Killian O'Sullivan from *Fair City*, and many of the glitterati of the music world, including the new Irish boy band Zoo, who were managed by Niall.

Niall's house was amazing. He had a full wall of expensive wines and champagnes. He had a hot tub in his back garden and many important decisions were made and banter was had sitting in the hot tub with a glass of Prosecco in hand. He was the kind of person I never believed would look at me for friendship and yet he accepted me into his circle. He gave me confidence at a time when I was struggling to fit in to the media circle, and for that I'll always be grateful. Sadly, Niall passed away a few years ago and his funeral was so packed I couldn't even get into the church. He was a man loved by many and missed by more. Another bright light switched off.

Throughout my career I have achieved some massive highs.

I became friends with stars in the music industry, record industry, music bosses, PR gurus, actors, managers – all people I felt beneath and never thought would even acknowledge me, let alone spend time with me. But I was part of something special for my years in RTÉ and it made me feel good.

I interviewed the big names, so many that I'd be here all day trying to name them all. One of my star-struck moments was backstage at the O2 (now the 3Arena) after I had been to see Lionel Richie perform. I had been obsessed with Lionel for years. I stood and sang at the top of my voice throughout the concert and, at the end, retreated to the VIP bar backstage. It was there that I saw Lionel – he was close enough to touch. I remember feeling giddy and I shouted to him, 'Lionel, Lionel, I love you so much. I just want to wrap you in a blanket and sing to you.'

He turned and looked at me, but before he could reply his security stepped in and said, 'I think it's time to go, Mr Richie.'

I think his bodyguard was petrified that I would lunge at him and attempt to swaddle him.

The only other time I remember being properly star-struck was when I interviewed Angie Stone for SPIN 1038 back in the early days. I walked into the foyer of the Morrison Hotel and I was instantly drawn to her. She had this massive personality and her aura shone brightly. Her presence literally took my breath away.

Another highlight was the time I was invited to one of *The X Factor* live shows by Louis Walsh. I felt so important, walking past the queue to head for the guest-list entrance, saying

'I'm on Louis' list.' It filled me with pride. This was the year that Ruth Lorenzo was taking part in *The X Factor* and when she sang the hair stood up on the back of my neck. She was awesome. Backstage, after the show, I managed to tell her that and she was so humble and grateful. I also briefly saw Simon Cowell as he swept by Louis' dressing room, shouting something humorous in Louis' direction.

Louis then brought me to the backstage bar before he went off to do some interviews. All of the acts were there and so were stars from TV in the UK, such as Ant and Dec. Now, this was unbelievable, as I had watched them on television from the time they presented *SMTV Live*, the ITV Saturday morning children's programme. I had followed them as they climbed the ladder to become the best TV presenters, I believe, the UK has ever seen. I went over and shook their hands and fangirled, telling them how amazing I thought they were. They were so sweet and Ant introduced me to his girlfriend, who is now his wife.

Other extreme highs in my career included times where I deejayed and emceed for top stars like George Michael and Anastacia, keeping their audiences in high spirits and building up the atmosphere for their arrival on stage. I also interviewed many big names on the radio and TV. I even had my own TV show for a while. No one I knew ever watched it, although, in fairness, I only presented it for eight months and it was on Sunday mornings at 10 a.m. It was called *SMS* (*Sunday Morning Show*) and while I had, at first, simply been covering for Laura Woods while she was off presenting another show,

I ended up getting the gig when Laura stayed on that other show. My presenting the show was an accident, really; I never went looking for work on TV. I'd been a guest on a lot of TV shows like *Seoige and O'Shea* and *The Afternoon Show* – but I'd never been alone on screen; it had never been just me. It was a whole new world, but I found that I thoroughly enjoyed it while I was doing it.

It was through working on the television side of things that I got to meet people like Aidan Power and Baz Ashmawy, as well as Michael Hayes and Mark O'Neill, who were in *How Low Can You Go?* They were all the nicest people that you could meet. It was also on TV that I met Kevin O'Connell, who I recognised as the guy from *The Late Late Toy Show*. I remembered when I was a kid, watching him doing the book reviews with Gay Byrne. He had progressed to working with Andy Ruane on *Scratch Saturday* and then moved on to his own shows. It turned out that he now directed *SMS* and I couldn't believe such a great presenter was my director.

Working in TV meant I had my own personal stylist. They would take me shopping for outfits to wear on the show and every Saturday before we recorded I would have my hair and makeup done in the beauty parlour backstage. At this time I had a lovely thin shape and had a short-lived burst of confidence. I was also thrilled at how my profile was really starting to grow.

However, all I had achieved over the last few years up to 2006 still seemed surreal. Despite my success, I continued to see myself as this small, useless being. I felt like I was pretending and that any day the important people would realise their mistake and ban this imposter from their world.

15

FUELLED BY PETROL

Unexpressed emotions will never die. They are buried alive and will come forth later in uglier ways.

Sigmund Freud

I had a huge passion for cars and rallying as I grew up. I used to have posters of cars up in my room and, as most pictures of cars had women draped over them, my parents thought for a while that I was gay and that putting the posters up was my way of letting them know! I managed to navigate in a few rallies in my twenties after I had attained my navigation licence, which legally allows you to take part. The navigator acts as the eyes of the rally driver, calling out the path ahead through notes. The thrill I felt powering through the countryside was like nothing I'd ever felt before.

I had a call in 2007 from Mick Bracken, owner of On The Limit Sports. His company recorded footage at all the major rallies and he was planning to produce a new show that would be packaged and broadcast on Motors TV and TG4. He wanted me as a presenter and I was delighted to accept the offer.

I was working seven days a week and couldn't have been

happier. My personal life was ignored as my professional life took over. I got a nomination for the Meteor Ireland Music Awards, the most prestigious awards ceremony in the country for Irish bands and artists. I had been put forward for DJ of the Year. As the awards ceremony came closer, I was pumped. I brought my mother and her best friend, Ann Quinn, to the ceremony. They had an amazing time, and came with myself and my friends Paul and Dev to Lillie's Bordello afterwards, where they mixed with some of the biggest names from Irish media.

I didn't win the award but came a close second to Ray D'Arcy. I couldn't have asked for better than that, really, as there had been some very big names in the mix. As Ray D'Arcy stood on stage he wished me the best. His acknowledgement was priceless to me – I felt as good as if I had won the prize.

It was during times like these that my illness was harder to notice. The lows were there but they were masked by the very real highs that I was experiencing in my career. The problem was, I never knew when to stop. Looking back I can see that this was when the emotionally unstable part of me really came to the fore. I would go to an after-party and by morning people would begin to filter home – but not me – I'd rally some followers and continue on to an early bar or back to mine. I kept fuelling myself with alcohol, and around this time I also began abusing prescription and class A drugs. Everyone seemed to be doing it. We were in the 'Boom Times' and money was never an issue. I don't know how I survived this period, as I spent the guts of two years living on alcohol, cocaine and takeaways.

Paul Byrne became my minder during this period. Paul is one of my closest friends. We met working on pirate radio around 2000 and instantly bonded. He would come with me to all the parties and events – he would usually be the one to make sure that I got home safely and coax me to call time when I'd had too much. I could always rely on him to have my back and keep me safe, no matter how crazy the situation.

I have only a fuzzy recollection of that time in my life due to the mood swings, the highs and lows, and the substance abuse. In fact Paul has now become something of a memory stick for my twenties. He tells me stories, like the time I turned down a dinner invite from Anastacia after her gig. Paul was there by my side through the entire time and sometimes when he tells me the stories I feel like he is telling me things about someone else's life. I can recall these things when he talks about them, but I am emotionally detached from them. I owe my life to him, really, as he always made sure that I was safe and unharmed, no matter how extreme the situation. He has remained a lifelong friend having been with me through the highs and lows, as have Audrey, Dev, Trolley and Thelma.

I met Dev, i.e. Ronan Devitt, at the same time that I met Paul, when working at the pirate station. He's one of my closest friends. He and Paul became like brothers to me, and when Paul introduced me to Glen Scanlon, aka DJ Trolley, he was added to the family – my three brothers. I could always rely on them and they could always rely on me. They remain close friends to this day.

16

HINDSIGHT

Although sometimes when the weight of the problem is more than enough for you to bear you feel the need to share, do so. There's nothing more heartening than a few comforting words from family and friends.

Unknown

My job as a DJ took me on the road a lot, as with my show, *The All Request Lunch* on 2FM, we would often broadcast from somewhere outside Dublin. As a result I always had somewhere new to go out for the night and there was always a party to attend. I was living the life and loving the music, oblivious to the fact that I was eroding my sanity a little every day.

I partied with the best. I worked with the best. I featured on the Witness Music Festival line-up and Creamfields in Fairyhouse. I was a name that could command an audience and I played up to the image of a successful DJ. I was unpredictable and controversial. I deejayed at Freshers' Week parties and college graduations. I would play music, climb up on the main speakers and have someone stand over me with a bottle of vodka, pouring it down my throat. I would always host the after-party in my hotel room.

I hosted one after-party for the American singer Akon after I had opened for him at the O2 Arena. It was back at a hotel in Co. Meath. We had the whole floor booked out. Akon, his crew, as well as DJs and home-grown acts that I knew all came along. It was a wild night and one that stands out for excessive highs. There were people walking around like zombies, with copious amounts of alcohol being drunk.

A lot of people don't know that BPD is closely paired with 'dual diagnosis' (the condition whereby one suffers from a mental illness and a substance abuse problem at the same time). Therefore alcohol and narcotics can often feature in the life of the sufferer. The relationship between BPD and addiction is a volatile one. Those who have BPD are more likely to engage in drug or alcohol consumption as an attempt to numb the pain. But the use of drugs and alcohol can aggravate some of the more dangerous symptoms of BPD, most notably rage and depression. So the life I was leading was playing into a growing illness that – you must remember – was still undiagnosed at this stage.

I was at every event, on every VIP list and stayed at the best hotels. My work lifestyle contributed to the public image I had as a party girl, the one with no worries, living the dream. But in truth, I lived wage packet to wage packet because I spent money on everyone else and on senseless parties. There were times when in my head I was encouraging myself to end my life but on the surface everything seemed fine as I was outwardly living the high life.

I'm out of control.

Please help me.

'The tab's on me – order what you want.'

It was around this time that I started getting myself into debt. People asked me for certain things. If I couldn't source them through work, I would purchase them and pretend I had gotten them for nothing. My public persona was that of someone who had everything and I felt I needed to become increasingly lavish to make that perception of me actually come true. I couldn't stop it. Giving someone what they asked for meant that they were nice to me, that they would shower me with attention. I convinced myself it'd be grand, I'd make the money back somewhere along the line. But I never did. I just fell further and further into debt, and further into the dark side of my mind.

Plotting my death became normal for me. It was something I thought about a lot. I knew how to do it, what to write in my suicide note. I even knew how I wanted my funeral to go.

17

DEATH BECAME ME

I didn't want to wake up. I was having a much better time asleep. And that's really sad. It was almost like a reverse nightmare, like when you wake up from a nightmare you're so relieved. I woke up into a nightmare.

Ned Vizinni, *It's Kind of a Funny Story*

Death was something that consumed my life for a number of years. It began with my grandfather's death in 2006. Hubert was a stern man and extremely regimented, but his approval was something I had always looked for. It came when I started to work for RTÉ. He would call me on the phone, especially in the weeks leading up to his death from oesophageal cancer. He would tell me how proud he was and, unusually, he confided in me about his anxiety of dying and leaving my grandmother behind, as she was suffering from dementia. He connected with me, he accepted me and then he died.

I remember the funeral cortege stopping by their cottage on the way to the graveyard. Nanny stood in the porch, watching, and asked her nurse 'Is that Hubert?' A shocked sadness crossed her face when the nurse nodded.

That night I was on *The Late Late Show* with Pat Kenny. (Yes, this is another example of my typical routine of extreme lows to highs.) I was on with my dog Fred. It was a piece on dogs wearing clothes and I had Fred dressed in a tux. I laughed and had fun with the other guests and their pampered pooches. No one would have guessed that I had just lost my grandfather.

After the show I drove to Co. Wexford and drank myself into oblivion at a friend's sister's wedding. I remember sitting on the balcony in my hotel room, watching the fireworks and crying my eyes out. I rang down to the reception. 'Could I have another bottle of wine sent to my room, please?'

When I was intoxicated I could sometimes pretend to myself that everything was okay. But I could also get angry with myself, sometimes smashing my fist or head against a wall, making sure I inflicted some level of pain on my horrible self. I was acting exactly how I felt I deserved towards myself – angry and willing to inflict pain. I would never direct this towards anyone else, just me.

You deserve it. You are a piece of shit!

18

DANCE WITH MY FATHER

Anger's like a battery that leaks acid right out of me.
And it starts in the heart 'til it reaches my outer me.

Criss Jami, *Venus in Arms*

Losing my father in 2007 was my most crippling moment. He'd been battling cancer for nearly ten years. He'd had some time in remission but the tumour came back, more aggressive than before. He fought as hard as he could and had chemotherapy until the doctors refused to give him any more. In the end he became very ill and was in and out of hospice care for months.

I knew my dad was sick, but dying? No. He'd be grand, sure who'd look after me otherwise?

No matter what arguments or disagreements my father and I had had in my youth, he had always soothed me by telling me that I was his favourite. He treated me to things I couldn't afford, like my first car when I was seventeen, and trips to London to see musicals. I never fully knew why he understood me when everyone else saw me as irrational and dramatic, but I suspect that it had something to do with the fact that he too had to fight his own mental battle, with alcohol. It was a battle I would say that he largely won, and at the time of his death in 2007 he had been off drink for twenty-four years. But, although it was never discussed when he was alive, he often suffered from panic attacks as a result of living with addiction. He never drank again after he came out of the Rutland Centre when I was four years old, but he did take on other addictions, like needing to buy twenty packets of Juicy Fruit chewing gum, or bags and bags of fruit gums. I think this addictive part of my father allowed him to identify with me a lot more easily than others.

I visited my dad when he was in the hospice and when he was out I would drive him where he needed to go. Eventually, his tumour became so aggressive that it burst through his abdominal wall and grew on the outside. As a result he smelled of rotting flesh. When the bandages were opened, so the wound could be cleaned, the smell was overpowering.

Although he was stubborn and wouldn't give up the fight, it was one he couldn't win. I'll never forget the day we were all called in to say our goodbyes. Dad lay in his hospice bed, unconscious, the morphine pump beeping beside him. The doctor told me that even though he wasn't conscious he would still be able to hear me. I'll never know if that was true or not. I knew he'd be worrying about me, though, so even in that moment I lied.

'I'll be okay, Daddy. Don't worry about me, I'll be okay.'

But in all honesty, I had no idea how I'd go on without him.

My sister Caroline and I decided we wanted to remember him as he was and not see him pass, so we left the hospice after saying our goodbyes. I cried as I drove back to Bray. There were a million things I wanted to say, but most of all: 'Don't leave me. Please don't leave me.'

Realising that no matter how hard you want something, or wish for it, it's not going to come true is a hard thing to swallow. They said it would take twenty-four hours until he let go. He lasted forty-eight.

8:30 a.m. 19 May 2007. My phone rang.

'Daddy's dead,' my brother told me.

The whole time I was in the funeral home with him I stood with my hands on his. I didn't take my eyes off him for a second.

Daddy, just wink and let me know you're in there. Give me a sign, anything, please.

Nothing.

In order to cope I went into organisational mode. I planned his funeral, booked a reception after the church and even wrote and delivered the eulogy. I put my grief to the back of my mind and made sure I was the 'Hostess with the Mostess'. I ensured that we gave him a good send-off.

I don't remember much about the time around and after my father's death. I was back to work the week after the funeral and back presenting *The All Request Lunch*, one of the most listened to shows in the country. I stuck on my 'I'm grand' face and got on with work, life and living. Within a couple of weeks I was acting like nothing had happened – not like I had lost the closest person to me in the world.

Looking back, I think I was in denial. I felt that if I didn't believe it, then maybe it hadn't really happened. Maybe we just hadn't spoken for a while? *That's it – he's been busy, I've been busy. Life's great.*

19

ANGELS

A person's a person, no matter how small.

Dr Seuss, *Horton Hears a Who!*

Caroline was expecting a baby in July 2007 – weeks after dad had died. This baby was our ray of light, our hope – the reason for my family to look forward. Luckily, my dad had already seen the new baby as Caroline had shown a 3D scan to him on his TV in the hospice.

The baby arrived on time. It was a boy and she named him Luke Patrick – the 'Patrick' was after my dad.

I invested everything emotionally into this new addition to our family. I offered to take him at every opportunity: to feed, to babysit, to walk – anything. He was the miracle that was going to dispel the sadness in our family. He was the one.

I quickly came to idolise Luke because we'd had so much sorrow with the death of not only my granda and father, but my uncle, two friends of mine – and Hollie.

My beautiful niece Hollie. She never took a single breath in this world but I remember every inch of her. Caroline and her partner had decided to take Hollie home to my parents' house to say goodbye. It was perfect. She was perfect. Same nose as our family, big feet like Caroline and the most beautiful rosebud lips. She smelled like a new baby, she felt like a new baby. I howled inside when I saw her.

Wake up Hollie, it's okay.

My heart was torn apart as my little sister had to say goodbye to her baby before she even got to say hello. The coffin was small enough to sit on her father's lap.

Later, I remember the respectful pause in traffic as we walked the short few minutes from the church to the graveyard to lay her to rest, the shocked faces as passers-by saw how small the coffin was. Hollie was an angel who will never, ever leave my heart.

Luke's birth was the first piece of good news the family had had in years, so everyone was over the moon to see him arrive – especially his parents.

One day, when I was visiting them, they sat me down and said, 'We'd like you to be godmother.'

My heart soared. 'I'm honoured. I promise I'll never ever let you down!'

Read that back – *I promise I'll never ever let you down*. That's quite a big promise to make.

Caught in the midst of an undiagnosed mental illness – as well as being in the grip of grief – I took the words literally and started to devote every waking hour to thinking about what I could do to make Luke's life better. I liked to spoil him and those around him. On the day of his christening, I organised food and drink for everyone. 'It's the least I can do for my godson,' I said, glowing. He wasn't just my nephew, he was my godson.

Now clearly Caroline and her fiancé, Darren, did everything for him, but a part of me believed I needed to be hands on. I ran to do anything at all that they asked. And I would not only do whatever task was required, but I would aim to do it better than even I thought I could. The goals I set myself were high – too high, really – but with my moods at a heightened state I pushed myself on and on and on. Never to let him down, that had been the promise.

20

ANOTHER HERO

Let us all meet each other with a smile, for the smile is the beginning of love.

Mother Teresa

A few months later, in September 2007, I felt my work and life balance was just right as I made my annual pilgrimage to the National Ploughing Championships. I was broadcasting live from the event and one of the perks of the job meant that I was staying in the penthouse of the nearby Hodson Bay Hotel. Sometimes, looking at the perks of my job, I couldn't believe how lucky I was. I still didn't think I deserved it, even while it was happening. It felt like I was living someone else's life – and the truth is that I was. I was living the life of one of my personalities; I was peeking out from under one of my many masks.

After breakfast on the morning of the broadcast my producer, Pat Morley, and I walked out the side entrance of the hotel and climbed a little grass hill to a helipad.

'Seriously?' I asked.

'Yes,' he smiled.

A friend of mine, whom I had met in Africa on a charity-related visit, happened to own helicopters and he had offered to fly us in. I felt pretty awesome, truth be told. My fellow broadcaster, Gerry Ryan, whom I held in very high esteem, had flown in before me and now here I was coming after him in my friend's chopper.

After we landed, we headed straight to the RTÉ tent and got ready to broadcast. I loved the ploughing championships because you got to meet so many listeners and people from all parts of the country in one place. It was great fun and we used to have great banter with the guys from the Garda Traffic Core, as well as the different stall owners, who were selling everything from wellies and ponchos to artisan food. It was the kind of festival I loved to be at; every year I put my hand up straight away when they asked for volunteers to broadcast from there.

Gerry Ryan was broadcasting before us on the morning of 26 September 2007. I sat in the road-caster (the station's mobile studio) and got things ready for my broadcast. When the news at the top of the hour came on, the presenter was talking about a major fire in my hometown of Bray. Caroline's fiancé's dad was a fireman in Bray. I texted her to see if she knew where it was happening:

> Hey, is Brian at that fire in Bray, where is it, they said near Superquinn

Nothing.

Something didn't sit right with me, particularly when the next news bulletin mentioned that a firefighter had been injured.

> Hey dunno if you are getting these with signal here. Is Brian at that fire in Bray?

Nothing.

I called. It went straight to voicemail.

I called Darren, Caroline's fiancé. Straight to voicemail.

Something felt wrong. I heard then that two firefighters had been killed. I felt panicked.

I turned to Pat Morley in the road-caster. 'It's my sister's fiancé's dad.'

'What is?'

'The fire. He's dead and I can't get in touch with my sister.'

I then texted Brian junior, Darren's brother. Nothing.

My mood was swinging quite dramatically as I tried to contact my sister in between smiling for photos, interviewing various people at the ploughing championship and being serenaded by Richie Kavanagh.

'Nikki, have you ever took a ride, ever took a ride … in a tractor?' Richie crooned.

Everyone sang along as I glanced at my phone.

Nothing.

The next news bulletin hit and I'd had enough. I knew where Brian junior worked in Kilmacanogue, so I rang directory enquires and they connected me to his office. I asked to speak with him. His manager answered: 'I'm afraid he's not here. He's had to leave. Can I help?'

'I'm his brother's fiancée's sister – it's Brian, isn't it? In the fire. I can't get my sister.'

'Yes it is, I'm sorry. I don't think they can reach his brother though,' the manager added.

I hung up and texted Brian junior again. My phone rang and I jumped onto it before the first ring finished. It was him.

'Brian – is it your dad? I'm hearing all sorts on the news.'

He cut over me. 'Where's Caroline?'

'I don't know, I've been trying to get her,' I replied.

'I think they said something about bringing Luke to Gorey for a swim, but I'm not sure – Darren doesn't know that dad's been killed.' Brian sounded panicked.

Holy hell – Caroline and Darren were most likely swimming with their twelve-week-old son, oblivious to the horror that had unfolded. I looked out the window of the road-caster at school kids laughing and running after each other in and out of the stalls.

I needed to find them. I had to do this. This was my one and only mission today. They weren't answering their phones. My sister listened to East Coast FM, so I called the newsroom and explained the situation. They put out an alert in the bulletins.

'Could Caroline O'Keeffe and Darren Murray please contact a member of your family or the gardaí as a matter of urgency.'

The grief of losing Hollie the year before had brought our families together. Supporting Darren and Caroline through that difficult period had allowed us to get to know each other. Darren's family had attended my father's funeral and when Luke was born we all celebrated together. Now here we were, four months almost to the day since my father passed, and we were trying to support Darren as his father was so tragically taken in the line of duty.

Luke had lost both his grandfathers in the space of four months.

The following evening I drove to Mary's house (Brian's grieving widow) for the wake. Mary had always been full of jokes and laughter, but that evening she was a very different person, consumed with shock and sadness and surrounded by her fifteen children – the youngest at the time being only three years old.

I blessed myself beside the coffin, which was positioned alongside the wall in the living-room, said a prayer and then watched as other family members, neighbours and friends arrived to offer their condolences and support. I felt shell-shocked. What was going on? It felt like everywhere I looked there was death and tragedy.

A hero who shouldn't be gone, Brian was laid to rest in between his own late daughter and my niece Hollie.

21

FORGOTTEN

The woods are lovely, dark and deep,
But I have promises to keep,
And miles to go before I sleep ...

Robert Frost, 'Stopping by Woods on a Snowy Evening'

Before Christmas I went to see my nanny, who was in a nursing home in Dunfanaghy in Co. Donegal. Because of her dementia, she'd been there since my granda passed. When I arrived at the home she had no idea who I was.

'I'm Ann's daughter.'

'Who's Ann?'

'I'm Eimear.'

'Where's Hubert?'

'Gone to the shops,' I replied. (We'd learned not to bring the grief avalanching back in on her.)

She didn't seem to remember much of anything. It's so hard to understand how someone could forget everything, but that is what dementia does.

'Are you Eimear?'

I felt hope, the prospect of recognition, an emotional reunion with my grandmother.

'Yes, Nanny.'

'Oh, the one off the radio.'

What?

It turned out that the nurses knew my job and had spoken to her whenever I came on the radio, telling her that that was her granddaughter. Sitting with her now, she remembered where I worked but not who I was in relation to her.

I had been very close to my grandmother growing up. I spent most of the summer holidays with my grandparents, picking veg from their garden, helping my nanny with cooking and tidying. She was warm and maternal and I loved her. Leaving the nursing home that day I grieved for another role model lost to the vast darkness.

Nanny passed away not long after that visit from the MRSA superbug. Another horrific death, another closed coffin. My mother was hit really hard by her death. While caring for my father during his final illness, she seemed to feel that she'd neglected her own parents in their time of need. This was not the case at all, as every spare moment she had was spent driving up and down the N2 from Dublin to Donegal. She cut herself into too many parts – she cared for my father and visited her mother and father as much as possible, while working full time to support the family.

It was bitterly cold the day of Nanny's removal to the house. It lashed rain, the drops feeling like they were cutting through my skin. I had a work commitment not far from the house, which I hadn't had time to cancel. I had been booked to put on a themed night in a local nightclub at the Seaview Hotel in Bunbeg. When I mentioned to my mother that I would have to let them know I couldn't do it, she responded that there was no point. 'Do it and just come back to the house. Sure it's only down the road.'

I booked myself a room in the hotel and that night I put on my mask, the heaviest mask of all. DJ Nikki Hayes. I showed up to the Seaview and it turned out to be an immensely successful night. The club was sold out and the owners were high-fiving me and at the same time offering their condolences. Afterwards, I ordered two bottles of wine and went to bed.

Waking up the following morning wasn't difficult. I fell into my clothes and drove the short distance to my grandparents' house. Cousins of my mother, people who said they were cousins of mine, all filed through the house.

'Oh, is this Nikki?'

'Hello, Nikki.'

Hello? What? I was Eimear, not Nikki, and my grandmother was lying dead in that coffin, which was closed because she had been ravaged in her final days by the MRSA bug. I had no time to put on my stage persona; I was grieving. But still I swallowed my frustration, my sadness and grief. I adjusted my mask so it glistened in the light.

'Yes, hi.'

Later that day, I delivered the eulogy. I performed as expected, although I wavered in my delivery. 'Two days ago Nanny stepped into Granda's arms where she will stay loved and protected forever.' My voice shook with emotion – this wasn't me, why was I letting everyone down? Anger rose as I swallowed my grief – get this done!

The morning after, the front page of the tabloids screamed, 'Nikki Hayes parties miles from where her grandmother lay in wake.'

I was horrified. Everyone would think I was cold and callous. But then a part of me began to believe the headlines. I started to think to myself, *Why would you be this person? How could you be so cold?* I was disgusted with myself. That night, I made deep cuts into my arms, which released the feelings of anger and shame about how I'd let my family down.

I spent the next month wearing long sleeves to hide the Picasso I'd carved on my skin.

22

OVERWHELMED WITH SUPPORT

I know what it's like to be afraid of your own mind.

Dr Spencer Reid, *Criminal Minds*

One day, shortly after the devastating tabloid headlines, I remember Gerry Ryan coming over to me. His desk wasn't too far from where I sat in the 2FM office but, since I had the highest respect for the man, I would never have dared burden him by being in his way or even in his eyeline. But he sought me out that day, popping his head around the desk separator surrounding my desk.

'You're a brave woman,' he said. 'Fair play to you.'

I broke into a sweat. Gerry Ryan was talking to me. I looked up, my eyes wide open; I felt panicked and more than a little star-struck.

'Don't mind anyone else bar you and your family. Work and the rest come behind,' he said.

Then he put his arms around me, kissed my head and walked away.

I was gobsmacked. These were the moments within the entertainment industry that people rarely saw and I was always humbled by. Gerry Ryan had reached out to me. I had become good friends with his brother, Mick, but Gerry was a god and I couldn't believe how nice he'd been to horrible, insignificant me, particularly as I had been having a tough time, trying to deal with my father's death and still maintain my work–life balance. There was also the fact that I'd once again been rapidly losing the will to live.

I saw people like Gerry as naturally belonging in the media, whereas I was a fraud and a passer-by. I always felt I didn't belong but had simply managed to sneak in the back door.

I was lucky to have the support of Gerry and other colleagues during that difficult time, but the people I worked with remained unaware of the fact that I had an illness, and I was determined to never show my true feelings in their presence. Some things that happened to me show that I must have succeeded.

I remember going to Cois Fharraige, a great music festival in Kilkee, Co. Clare, about a year or so after my father's death. I asked my mum to come with me as she was home a lot on her own. Perhaps I also wanted to show off my position as a broadcaster in the hope that she would be proud of me. All the industry heads were there and everything was free, including a complimentary suite in Doonbeg Castle with meals and festival access. The suite was amazing. Beautiful décor, four-poster beds and beautiful views.

A few friends of mine were attending the festival too, so

I met up with them at the venue. The Blizzards were rocking it out to the afternoon's spirited crowd. The crowd was really starting to build and the atmosphere was good. My mother appeared to feel out of her comfort zone, however, as it wasn't really her scene. Seeing her discomfort, I felt I needed to mind her, so I brought her around to meet some people. After a while she seemed to start enjoying the gig, shaking her hips ever so slightly as The Blizzard's Niall Breslin belted out 'Fantasy'.

That evening we were invited to have dinner in Doonbeg with the rest of the assembled media. There were many senior figures within the industry present, as well as people who had come onto the scene around the same time as me.

There were a couple of people whose names I would've mentioned at home over the years, so I set to doing the introductions.

'Mum, this is Tony. This is Martin.' Etcetera, etcetera.

I took her right around the room. We were about to take our seats for food with two friends of mine, when a DJ that my mum listened to came into my eyeline. When I pointed him out she seemed eager to say hello and so I took her over and introduced her to the people at the table. I was surprised and hurt when one of them blatantly turned around and ignored me. It felt like I'd been hit with a bat in the face. As I walked away, trying to limit any further damage to my dignity, I heard him follow up with, 'That one thinks she's something. Well let me tell you, she's far from it.'

I couldn't understand it. It's true that we had never been best friends, but I couldn't believe he would humiliate me so cruelly in front of my mother. I felt ridiculed and barely touched my dinner.

Later on, after my mom had gone to bed, my two friends decided to come up to the sitting-room in the suite and have a drink. They mentioned the elephant in the room immediately.

'What was he doing? That was so awkward!'

'I don't know,' I smiled.

But I wasn't smiling on the inside, oh no; I was feeling out of control. I needed to release the pain from my body. Eventually the lads crashed on the sofa. When I was sure they were asleep I went to the kitchenette of the suite, picked up a large sharp knife and stabbed myself in the leg. When I cut myself it was like I could feel the negative emotions escaping from my body. It gave me peace, serenity. In that moment, post-harm, I felt at one with the world.

This time, however, after that initial glow, I got a fright as I realised that I could see right into the cut. It was white. I started to panic. *What have I done?* The wound looked like it needed urgent medical attention.

I woke up one of the guys and showed him the wound. At the sight of it he got sick a little, but then we both went into fix-it mode. I got shoeshine cloths from the vanity set and ran them under the water and added salt to sterilise the wound. I managed to find bandages in my bag. I placed the shoeshine cloth, now soaked in salt, onto the surface of the wound. I placed a face-towel over that and then I wrapped the bandages around my thigh to form a makeshift dressing. It was only when the bleeding didn't stop that I drove to a local pharmacy and bought Steri-Strips. I knew from previous incidents that they helped deep cuts to heal faster.

Thankfully my mother didn't hear a thing throughout the night and, as I had become the master of deception, she was none the wiser about the fact that while I drove us home the following day I was in excruciating pain with my thigh lacerated and throbbing. Despite the pain I never went near a doctor – the wound healed over time, but I was very lucky that it didn't become infected.

Shortly after this, my mother emigrated to America. She sold the family home in Bray and moved to Florida to be near my sister Ann-Marie and her family. Ann-Marie had moved there a year after 9/11. By that time she was in her second marriage, to a lovely NYPD cop called Tommy, who is a typical big-hearted New Yorker with Italian colouring and a broad Brooklyn drawl. They had a son, Conor, and after 9/11 they decided that they didn't want to raise him in New York so relocated to Florida, where in 2007 they had twin girls.

As for the person who snubbed me, he has no idea that what he said and did that night caused me to go to such extremes to punish myself. To this day he is still oblivious to the damage his words provoked.

23

RELEASING THE PAIN

Sick of crying,
Tired of trying.
Yes I'm smiling,
But inside I'm dying.

Unknown

I had been cutting for a while before the Doonbeg incident, and it continued afterwards. The urge to self harm tended to start with a feeling of anger towards myself and thoughts of how unworthy I was to be alive, as well as an anger that I hadn't done more with my dad while he was alive. This avalanche of hurt, guilt and despair drove me to cut myself slowly and painfully, making sure every drop of blood came with meaning. I was overwhelmed, I was frightened. I had no one. I couldn't stop the thoughts racing in my head:

You're no one.

I want my Daddy.

You didn't deserve him.

He's never coming back.

Because I was so reliant on my father throughout his life,

I had been drowning in emotions since his death, yet I had refused to acknowledge them. But eventually they became too strong to ignore.

On one occasion I cut myself when I got home to my place after presenting my show. I was living in Baltinglass at the time. In the 'Boom Times' my father had convinced me that I needed to buy a house. To this day I have no idea why I chose a place in Co. Wicklow so far from Dublin, but I did, even though I knew no one in the area.

It was a Friday evening. I took out the knife and sat on the stairs. I ran the blade up and down my thighs knowing that if I leaned a little deeper I would get that blood-fall and relief I so desperately needed. I was wound up, anxious and stressed. I pressed the blade onto my thigh and started to cry. My cries quickly became sobs, sobs that turned to anger – immense anger directed inwards at the disgusting person I was.

I drew down on the blade and in a frenzy sliced at my thigh. Blood sprayed out and I quickly realised that I had caused too much damage. I would have to go to the hospital. But I had no one who was close enough to bring me. I was going to have to face this on my own.

I looked at my thigh and could see that I had sliced through the muscle. My only thought was about how to stem the bleed. I was already feeling light-headed. I knew I wasn't going to be able to tend to it like I had in Doonbeg, when I had salt, a roll of bandages and other makeshift dressings to hand. I grabbed the cord from my dressing gown and some kitchen roll. I wrapped my thigh in kitchen roll and cling film and pulled the dressing gown cord tight around the wound. I then wrapped it again with brown tape. I pulled up my trousers and went out to the car. I knew this was a temporary fix and so drove towards the nearest hospital, which was in Naas, praying my makeshift bandage would last until then.

I felt searing pain in my leg as I drove along the road. I must have been in shock, as I listened to the radio and even somehow answered a work phone call. There is no way the person on the other end of the phone that day could have envisaged the state I was in.

I drove the half hour to Naas General Hospital, pulled up in the car park and put money in the meter for parking. Then I limped into A&E. It was pretty busy, being a Friday evening, so I queued behind a few people in order to register with reception. I didn't have a doctor's referral, so I was informed that I would be charged for the visit.

'That's fine,' I said.

'So tell me, what's the problem?' the receptionist asked. She was mid-forties with glasses. I could tell they were just for reading, as they sat at the end of her nose. She had brown hair with highlights and a very business-like manner.

'I have a large laceration to my left thigh.'

'How did this happen?'

The receptionist looked at me as I hesitated. *Should I pretend or tell the truth?*

I took a deep breath. 'I did it to myself.'

She looked back at me, her eyes widening. She was silent for a moment. I think she suspected that I had made a mistake and was giving me the opportunity to correct myself. When I remained quiet, she sighed and said, 'Okay, sit down there and the triage nurse will see you soon.'

A nurse called me immediately. She was a lovely, smiley, middle-aged woman and she made me feel at ease. 'What have you managed to do here to yourself at all? Was it an accident?'

Do I lie and pretend or tell the truth?

'I did it to myself with a kitchen knife.'

She opened my makeshift bandage, which had managed to keep the flow to a minimum. The kitchen towel and cord were soaked in blood and the minute she removed them blood started spraying out like a squirting hose. She put pressure on the vein.

'Right so, let's get this cleaned up,' the nurse said matter-of-factly. 'You're going to need quite a few stitches here.' Her eyes still on the wound, she asked, 'Did you want to die or just hurt yourself?'

'I don't know, I just wanted to stop the pain.'

Stop the pain by causing pain. I didn't understand it myself, so I don't know how I expected a stranger to understand. She smiled at me and told me not to worry; they'd get me patched up and the psychiatrist on call would see me soon. She asked if I had anyone I'd like to call.

'No, thank you.'

I was transferred to a bed in A&E to await a doctor to stitch my thigh back together. Lying on the bed, I texted my friend Paul. I didn't mention where I was. Instead I chatted with him about the approaching weekend and the fact that plans we had made mightn't be a goer, as I'd hurt my leg. That's all I said. Paul knew I struggled with my mental health. He knew me better than most people in my life. At that moment, though, I didn't want to share what I'd done with anyone.

The doctor appeared about an hour after I was moved to the bed. She took off the bandages and my leg started gushing blood again. I was exhausted. She said she'd have to give me about twenty stitches.

'Can you numb the area, please? I don't want to feel the pain.'

She was a youngish doctor and she tried to keep the conversation light and breezy. She laughed. 'After what you did you want pain relief now?'

She didn't understand. It was different when I hurt myself. But this was someone else doing it and so I wanted to be numb.

I got a local anaesthetic and was patched up. I would have to go to my GP in a week's time, I was told, to have the stitches checked. They would be removed the week after.

It was 11 p.m. I wanted to go home, but I had to stay another hour until the psychiatrist on call saw me. I knew the drill. I knew that if I gave the right answers I would be allowed to go home.

'Did you want to hurt yourself?'

'No, I was upset and angry.'

'Did you want to die?'

'No, I got a fright. I cut deeper than I meant to.'

'Do you have any feelings of wanting to end your life now?'

'No.'

'Is someone able to come and pick you up?'

'Yes, my friend should be here in the next ten minutes.'

He agreed to let me go if I followed up with an outpatient appointment. I thanked him, thanked the nurses and limped out the door with a crutch they had given me to keep the weight off my leg. I got into the car and drove home. Once home, I fed the dogs and went to bed, exhausted but grateful for the pain relief they had provided.

24

I CAN'T HANDLE ME

Darkness cannot drive out darkness;
Only light can do that.
Hate cannot drive out hate;
Only love can do that.

Martin Luther King

After the horror of so many heartbreaking deaths in my family we had a break, but, for me, the real trouble was bubbling to the surface. About a year after my father died, I totally fell apart. Since just after his death I had been taking a light anti-depressant, more to help me sleep and curb my anxiety than anything else. My BPD was still undiagnosed, but I had been given a general diagnosis of being depressed. However, I had no follow-up appointments with a psychologist or a mental health representative, and I started to believe that I could better control my emotions without the medication. I convinced myself that the pills slowed me down; it made it seem like I couldn't feel anything. So I decided to stop taking this medication, abruptly and without any medical supervision.

Something had to give. I was working hard, travelling up

and down the country for broadcasts, and partying harder. I took as many extras shifts as possible and my alcohol consumption increased, as did the number of hangovers. This meant that I never had a second to actually deal with how I was feeling. The most important person to me, my dad, had died and I was in complete denial.

I have since learned that one of the repeated patterns of BPD sufferers is the use of distraction to avoid pain. When you are distracted you don't have to deal with the difficult thoughts and feelings – and you can pretend they'll just go away. Unfortunately it never works out that way, but this behaviour becomes programmed into our brains and to this day when I'm going through difficult times my default setting is to avoid reality and focus on unimportant matters.

Any time I did think about the reality of what had happened with my father, I felt I was losing control. My legs would shake, my jaw would tighten and my eyes would fill up – I would panic and lock the sadness away. I was afraid that if I showed it the light of day it would take over and consume me. I bottled up my feelings for so long, that twelve months after I buried my father I started to fragment and my vulnerability became obvious to those around me. Friends started noticing that I was out at least five days of the week. I'd lost weight, I was edgy; they later told me that they didn't know how to be around me and if my father was brought up in conversation they noticed I would quickly divert it elsewhere.

I pushed my family and friends away. I started to hang out with people who didn't ask about my father and didn't care.

They loved me for what I could give them and not for who I was. I bought friends because I liked to be needed and when I was needed I was accepted. I didn't want to be disliked or unloved so I did everything to keep unimportant people close and those who cared for me far away. This is known as emotional dysregulation and is a huge factor in BPD.

At the time I was earning a good wage but I was still stretched. Taking on the expenses of the new friends I'd met meant every penny I earned went right back out again. I was now emotionally and financially in trouble.

Then, one Friday, I booked myself a hotel room and locked myself away from the world for the entire weekend. I drank when I woke and didn't stop until I passed out again. No one came looking for me – friends and family had become so used to my withdrawal from their company that they didn't even question why I'd disappeared.

The floodgates opened that weekend. Intoxicated I allowed myself to dwell on my father's absence, the fact that he was never coming back to me. I felt the tears like acid stinging my eyes. I tried to call a friend for help but my jaw tightened. I could speak, but I didn't make sense. I curled up into the foetal position and sobbed so much that every ounce of strength or resolve disappeared. I wanted my daddy, I needed him.

When I eventually resurfaced after the weekend, I told my family where I'd been and what I'd done. I was distraught. I knew I needed help and my family asked my doctor to have me admitted to hospital. In all senses of the word, I was out of control.

My family felt hopeless, unable to help me. I was breaking, shattering and no one could help me. So I was sent to the professionals in St John of Gods. Once again faith and hope was placed in the mental health services. The hope that their expertise could in some way fix me and make me normal. But that didn't happen. Instead, I chose to leave the hospital and go back to my life pretending everything was okay.

I had worn so many masks for so many people that I no longer knew who I was. I felt like I was locked into a costume shop. I dressed up for every occasion and managed to be everything for everyone – except for myself.

I had hundreds of acquaintances, as with texts or social media I could be whoever anyone wanted me to be. But I found maintaining close friendships difficult. As for personal relationships, they were very messed up. I only ever dated long-term twice before my husband, Frank. One was a juvenile relationship, the other was toxic. In a messed-up way I felt if I became close to someone who walked all over me, hit me or abused me, this would confirm that the opinion I had of myself was correct. I was getting what I deserved. This was the same justification that I gave when I was cutting through my bare flesh and when I swallowed handfuls of pills all at once, or the time I stood on the side of a cliff in Bray the year after my father's death and thought that if I just jumped the pain and mental stress I was under would go away. Arms in the air, I had felt the exhilarating peace and silence that I would fall into, my pain over.

'People kill themselves not because they want to end their lives but because they want their pain to be over.'

Jim Morrison said that and it's true. When I'm suicidal, I only think of the here and now and the fact that I'm completely overwhelmed. I am screaming inside my head: *Help! Help! Please stop this!* Instead of communicating my desire for help and my fear of the thoughts that are building up in my head, however, I will offer a smile to the world and exhaust myself in a bid to make sure that everyone thinks I am okay.

I was in this sort of anguished headspace when, in 2010, after seven years with the company, I lost my job in RTÉ. I had some of the biggest highs in my career in Montrose. I presented my own TV show. I was at the helm of one of the country's biggest radio shows. I thought I was secure but one afternoon, shortly after I had finished presenting my three-hour show in our studios in Dundrum Town Centre, I was told that I had just finished my last show on 2FM. I wasn't on the new schedule.

My show producer at the time, Maggie Stapleton, and I were in shock. There was no warning. I hadn't done anything wrong. According to the JNLR (Joint National Listenership Research, which surveys the general public on their radio choices), my listenership figures were performing well. When, at a later time, my union rep questioned the decision, he was told that the station had decided to go for an older audience and that I didn't fit with that demographic.

I wasn't bitter one bit about how things ended with RTÉ. Hurt, yes. Upset, yes. But bitter – no. I already believed that I was not good enough in life, so I just saw what happened as more proof of this.

The loss of my job at 2FM exacerbated my self-worth problems. It was one of the most painful times in my life. When things were bad in my personal life, I always had Nikki, my stage persona. Now it seemed as if that had been taken from me as well and in a way that I didn't have any control over. But if I couldn't be Nikki then what – or who – could I be? Panic-stricken, I contemplated going to sleep and never waking up.

25

REGRETS

Hope is being able to see that there is light despite all of the darkness.

Desmond Tutu

When I am well I often feel sorry for myself. I see how much unnecessary pain I have dragged myself through, how many great friendships and connections I've destroyed. I isolated myself, yet often felt searing pain because I was so lonely. In my darkest days I would walk through Dublin city, surrounded by people laughing, heading to or from work, or chatting on their phones, and I would feel the pulse of my latest cut attempting to repair itself. Yet I couldn't repair what was inside, because I didn't know who I was.

Acceptance within my industry was always a huge thing for me. I knew a lot of people in media who came from privileged backgrounds and were glamorous and, in my opinion, stood on pedestals high above me. They were singers, actors and people whose careers I watched unfold as I grew up. I felt like a fraud in their company and when I was around them I would be loud, act in an overly friendly manner and spend the whole night massaging their egos – ones that weren't there to start with. I made people feel awkward because I was a stranger showering them with compliments.

When I first entered the serious side of broadcasting, working for SPIN, I instantly placed myself at the bottom rung of the ladder. I was working with top DJs like Johnny Moy and Emma Ledden from MTV. These people were royalty to me and I wondered how on earth I could ever reach their level. Both of them were sweethearts but I still felt that I should grovel at their feet. Years later, I spoke with Johnny and he couldn't believe that I ever felt that way.

When I moved to RTÉ my self-hatred was magnified, as I was working with legends like Larry Gogan and Rick O'Shea. I didn't just have these guys on a pedestal – I worshipped them. As a result, I never felt part of this privileged group. I was always at the bottom, looking up in bewilderment and wondering how on earth I got there. It was sheer dumb luck, that's what I'd tell myself. It had nothing to do with talent or personality.

As part of my job, I would often meet bands and interview them. After a few times interviewing them they would get to know me, or recognise me at least. Even though I may have interviewed the same person a million times, the next time I saw them I would extend my hand and say, 'Hi, I'm Nikki Hayes from 2FM.' In my mind, I believed there was no way they would remember me because I was so forgettable. Although I would often be met with something like, 'I recognise you, Nikki. How're things?', I would assume that they were just trying to be nice and so I would burn with shame, convinced they had taken pity on me.

When I was let go so publicly from 2FM, a large part of me felt that this was what I deserved. I had only been a pretender, anyway. The likes of me, a common girl from Bray, should never have been part of that world. No one liked me. I was a horrible human being. Once I was let go I really wanted to die. I needed a way of escaping from myself, and if I didn't have the luxury of switching into a new personality for work, I knew I would drown in my own darkness.

The day I was fired I drove for two hours, sobbing my heart out. My mind found it hard to process. This was something that had been a stable part of my life and now it was gone. I didn't know what I was going to do or how I was going to survive the public humiliation. I believed people would hear about my sacking and hate me more than they already did. I believed they would enjoy hearing the news and be glad that this was how things had turned out for me. I was at rock bottom and I didn't see how I was going to get through it all.

'Nikki Hayes is so fake.'

'Her voice grates my nerves. She's a fat asshole.'

These were the kind of things written about me on the popular public discussion forum boards.ie. All the negative comments tore into me. I started to become obsessed. I googled my name. It led to many online communities.

> Couldn't be happier they let that nikki hayes go. now lets see some real talent

> Yes there is a god nikki hayes is gone from 2FM

Some of the comments were a lot harsher than these examples. Any positives, such as 'Sorry to hear nikkis gone', were seen but quickly forgotten by me, of course, whereas the negatives surrounded me, like children in a playground, name-calling, and all I could do was cower in the corner of my mind as they continued to mock me.

I've said it so many times, but if it weren't for Louis Walsh, I wouldn't be here now. He had always been friendly to me but when I lost my job in 2FM so suddenly he swooped in to catch me before I crashed to the ground. He enlisted the wonderful Joanne Byrne and Sinead Ryan from Presence PR to advise me. Louis called me and motivated me to apply for other jobs. This was during a time when hibernating in my pyjamas was the one and only thing I wanted, other than to curl up and die. The only thing Louis would accept was my going back out to events and showing the world I was strong and not a mere puppet in the RTÉ chain of command.

One night he invited me to a Westlife concert, which was being broadcast live on Sky. When I was seated I saw that I was sitting behind Georgina Ahern, the wife of band member Nicky Byrne. She is another person who has always been kind and friendly any time we met.

The concert was brilliant. Halfway through the set, the boys were talking to the audience when Mark stood up and said, 'We want to dedicate this next song to a good friend of ours, Nikki Hayes, who has supported us from the very start. It's "Flying Without Wings".'

Without thinking, I started to clap along with everyone

else. It was only as people turned and looked at me that I realised what was happening. In the moment I hadn't absorbed that fact that it was to me they were dedicating one of their biggest songs. Once it sank in my jaw dropped and I felt like I was on top of the world.

After the gig, I went by their dressing room and thanked them. The boys in Westlife have always been so lovely to me throughout my career and I particularly connected with Mark. There is a song Westlife recorded for one of their albums that was never released as a single – although I had championed for them to do so. It was called 'Talk me Down' and Mark sang it solo. I had first heard it a few months earlier. The lyrics in that song made sense to me. I heard the cry for help. I felt the pain. The lyrics, particularly those about the 'crossfire in my head', described exactly the desperation and feeling of helplessness I had experienced that night in 2008 when I stood on the roof of a London hotel as my trapped self screamed for someone to help me. For me, it was my sister Ann-Marie and her husband who managed to talk me down, after I called them in desperation. They spoke to me, keeping me distracted until I got into bed and fell asleep.

I've explained to Mark how those lyrics and his voice connected with me when I didn't even know how to connect with my own soul. It will always remain a special song to me.

26

REFUGE

I've got ninety-nine problems and eighty-six of them are completely made up scenarios in my head that I'm stressing about for no logical reason.

Bill Murray

Losing my job hit me hard, but it also made me realise just how out of the way I was in Wicklow. I didn't have any friends in Baltinglass and, as I wasn't making the trip to Dublin every day for work, I became more and more isolated. So I made the decision to move back to Dublin. I moved to a one-bed flat in Kilmainham. It took me two days to move in and being back in the city took a few days, even weeks, to get used to. I was close to St James's Hospital, so all I could hear at all times of the day and night were sirens.

During my moving-in process, I called an old friend, Ollie, to tell him that I'd moved into the city centre. Ollie was always ready with a bottle or two of wine. He cooked for me and brought me basic things I hadn't gotten yet. Ollie had his own issues. He was in his forties and had lost a long-time partner to death. Once he had some alcohol in him, he would become very emotional and would end up crying. I was happy to be a sounding board for all his problems. He was the perfect friend for me at the time, as concentrating on someone else's issues and avoiding putting myself under the spotlight was exactly what I needed.

I cared for Ollie very much. We had parties, we went to drag shows and bingo. It was Ollie who first introduced me to the gay community in the city, which screamed acceptance and love and, once I joined, I never ever wanted to let it go.

I wasn't gay. I had kissed girls before but always with drink in me and never seriously. I did consider the fact that I might be bisexual at one stage but that turned out to just be my mood swings. I did have some confusing times when friendships with other women almost became relationships, but I was just lost and didn't know who I was – once again I was trying to be all things to all people.

I spent 2010–11 immersed in Dublin's gay community. I made friends. I went to all the gay nights out and always ended up having a great night where, unusually, I didn't feel like I had to hide behind a mask. I did feel wild, that nothing could stop me, that the city was mine – until Tuesday morning, when the weekend's toxic cocktail would catch up with me and I would be back knocking on the door of despair, while also smiling on the surface as I presented my new show, back on SPIN 1038.

Everyone was oblivious to the strain I was under during this period. I was suffering with panic attacks and anxiety a lot during those days, and in between those moments my disproportionate reactions were starting to take their toll. I felt so low and insignificant.

27

PUSHING AWAY WHAT I NEED

I don't think people understand how stressful it is to explain what's going on in your head when you don't understand it yourself.

Unknown

I remember when I was younger a few girls from my estate who I hung around with decided to choose their 'best friend' in the group. There were five of us and you can imagine who wasn't picked by anyone. Yes, me. That fuelled my already existent feelings of abandonment and exclusion. Most teenagers may have brushed off such a silly incident but I held onto this rejection, obsessed about it and let it harm me deep inside. All I could think was that everyone had a best friend except me – no one wanted me to be their best friend. To this day I can still feel the stabbing pain as all four girls celebrated their new best friend status and looked at me pityingly. I remember how I made my excuses and headed home to bury my head in a pillow and hold my breath until I gasped.

It is a symptom of BPD that the sufferers find it very difficult to make and maintain relationships, but of course I didn't know this at the time. As I grew older I began to develop a pattern of getting close – but not too close – to friends and acquaintances. I had friends everywhere, but if they got too close I would jump back and push them away. I grew to like keeping everyone at arm's length. I felt that by doing so it meant that I could be who they needed me to be without letting my mask slip. I panicked about what would happen if people got to know the real me. The fear of rejection and abandonment was colossal.

I believed that friendships only developed when I did whatever was needed of me and didn't ask for anything back. I know now that that's not a sustainable dynamic in any relationship, but it made sense to me then because I thought it kept my friends happy and me safe. My friends weren't happy at times, however, because people like to get to know you and enjoy your company. I ran hot and cold so much that no one really knew where they stood with me. But I didn't like to be challenged on this, so when this happened I retreated further and further away from the people who did.

I craved support and yet I ran from those who offered it. I felt like I was standing on a ledge with my arms outstretched; I wanted to step back to safety and yet always jumped off regardless. In the throes of undiagnosed BPD, I really believed that I was acting normally and it was everyone else who was off the ball.

My friendship with Thelma is a good example of this. I first met Thelma when I was hospitalised for anorexia in 1995. We were just two young, frightened girls in a psychiatric ward, surrounded by people suffering from numerous issues. She always laughs when she remembers our first introduction. I was in the bed next to her.

'Hi, I'm Eimear. I've anorexia. What are you here for?'

She was timid and sitting with her father. She smiled at me and in a low voice said, 'Bulimia.'

She is a beautiful soul and we became close during our hospital stay. When we were both discharged we stayed in touch. She would come to stay weekends at my house and I would stay at hers. I became very close to her family, especially her parents. Toddy was a man with a big, hearty laugh and strong handshake, and Geraldine, like Thelma, was softly spoken and kind. I became so close to Thelma that for a while I would stay in Wexford almost every weekend. As we got older, we would go out on the town and she noticed that I couldn't handle alcohol too well, that I went wild when I had a lot. And there wasn't a gradual build up. Instead it went from everything is all right straight to – bang – wildness. She spoke to me about it, but I was young and at the time liked the idea of being untameable and wild.

Thelma got pregnant young and when her beautiful little girl, Nykia, was born, I travelled down to the hospital in Wexford to see her. I'd never seen Thelma look so happy as she did that day. Nykia was adorable. I remember feeling very grown up, seeing my best friend with a baby. I deejayed at Nykia's christening and always loved visiting and playing aunty.

A few years after Nykia's birth Thelma suffered a great tragedy. Her mother had a freak accident while abroad and died.

I couldn't believe it when she called me. Kind, gentle Geraldine couldn't be dead. I drove to Wexford as soon as I finished work (I was doing some office temping at the time and working at Passion FM). Geraldine was a beautiful woman who had accepted me into her home as if I were her own. I still can't hear Shania Twain's 'Forever and For Always' without being transported back to the chapel with her coffin passing by me.

Thelma was such an important part of my life in those years. But we had a falling out a few years ago and things haven't been the same since. I was running around the country with my job (this was during my time in 2FM) and Thelma had met a great guy, Paul, who worshipped the ground she walked on and wanted to marry her. Thelma asked me to be one of her bridesmaids and I was over the moon. At the same time, I was finding it increasingly difficult to maintain relationships with people and so whenever she suggested dress shopping I found a reason not to go. It became so bad that, a month before her wedding, I hadn't shown up for one fitting. The dresses had been bought and I received a call from Thelma.

'Are you going to make the wedding?'

'Of course I am.' What a question to ask.

'You've let me down so much over the past year,' Thelma said, 'I don't know if I can trust you to turn up.'

She then told me she'd asked an old school friend to take my place and luckily she was the same size as they'd guesstimated for me.

My heart fell to the floor. I was gutted and broke down crying. I knew I had been unreliable and afraid to commit to anything. I could have made some of the dress fittings but I had convinced myself when they came up that I couldn't. However, instead of remaining remorseful and apologising I got angry.

'Paul never liked me anyway and you were always going to replace me.'

She didn't deserve that outburst and neither did Paul. I was feeling flashes of rage and was quite out of control. When I put the phone down my heart raced, my palms were sweaty and I started to shake all over.

What's happening to me?

I put my head between my knees until the shaking stopped and then went to bed, drew the curtains and rang in sick for the week. I camped out under my duvet. I felt worthless. I felt guilty. I hated myself and I needed to be punished. This time I didn't cut myself; I did something I'd never done before. I tied my belt into a loop, placed it around my neck and thought of all the places nearby I could jump from to break my neck. No more pain, no more letting people down, no more noise in my head. I didn't have the balls for it, though, so I took a mouthful of painkillers and went to sleep.

I am still friends with Thelma but our relationship is a lot more distant than it used to be. I love her and I know she loves me. I just let her down on the biggest day of her life and in the years surrounding it. Nykia is nearly eighteen now, which makes me feel so old. She is the image of Thelma at that age. (I see her updates on Instagram and it's like taking a trip back in time, as they are practically twins at that age.)

The few friendships that I still hold on to, I do so because those people know exactly who I am and don't expect what they know I can't give.

I see now, of course, that as a result of my self-imposed isolation, I lost out on friendships that would have enriched my life. Instead of trying to deal with the emotions that were crippling me, I withdrew myself from everyone and became a very lonely person. I spent all my time out of work locked in my house with my two dogs, Fred and Sandy. I knew everyone but no one knew me.

28

WORDS CRUSH ME

I'll draw you a picture, I'll draw it with a twist.
I'll draw it with a razor, I'll draw it on my wrist.

Linda Gonzales, 'I'll Draw you a Picture'

I remember being asked to host a beauty pageant in a top Dublin nightclub. This was a few months after losing my job on RTÉ so publicly and for no reason bar the want of a change. My confidence was low and I was really questioning my place in the entertainment industry.

I was doing the hosting for an old friend from Bray. I never said no to people who asked me for favours, as I felt it was my duty to give back. The thing was, I was often giving back to people that I had never taken from in the first place. I hadn't wanted to host this event as I had put on a lot of weight. I had also just started working again for SPIN 1038 and wasn't earning even half of what I had been on, so money was tight, which meant I couldn't afford an expensive outfit. However, that feeling that I owed people and needed to please them made me agree.

I was very nervous. I picked out a plain black dress, indistinct enough that it would make me fade behind the girls. I was hosting my worst nightmare: a beauty pageant. Beautiful girls would surround me, as I stood, obese, smiling beside them. I knocked back a few vodkas for courage and put on my smile.

Once the night started I relaxed. A friend of mine, Louise, a beautiful transgendered woman, had set up a photography business and I had arranged for her to take the photos at the event. I saw her running around doing the shots and I felt at ease knowing I had a friend nearby.

I had done many of these pageants so I knew what was expected. The girls were very sweet and very beautiful. I kept pressing down the hatred I felt towards myself. At the interval I had another drink and felt more relaxed. For the second half, I decided to have a bit of fun with the girls. I laughed and joked and even got heckled by the crowd. The atmosphere was great and everyone seemed to be having a good time.

Then things turned nasty. 'You fat, ugly gowl,' I heard one attendee say from where she stood near the stage. She looked straight at me.

I wanted to bolt, to run down the stairs and leave. I felt bile rise in my throat; I thought I was going to be sick. But I finished the interviews, smiling and laughing. I left as soon as it was all over and done with.

The following day I logged on to Facebook and saw I was tagged in a message:

> @nikkihayes is a crude disgusting mongo. Shamed for her.

It was the girl from the previous night who had abused me from the crowd. I tried to delete the message from my page but couldn't. I panicked. Now everyone was going to think that's how I was, that's who I was. I threw up. I went back to look at the girl who posted it. I can't remember now exactly who she was, but what I do remember very clearly is how her remark made me feel.

29

MY KNIGHT IN CAMOUFLAGE

Some souls just understand each other upon meeting.

N. R. Hart

Meeting Frank was one of the best things that ever happened to me. I remember I was making a guest appearance in a club in Donegal that night. He first approached me by messaging me on Facebook:

Fancy a drink later? youre in my neck of the woods.

Something made me stop and think about it, and I didn't know why. So I said yes.

Spookily, it turned out that Frank and I had lived part of our lives almost side by side without ever actually meeting. When in college in Donegal I had hung around with his brother, Michael. His cousin Emma was one of my college friends. I had even met his mother in my previous life in Letterkenny.

Of course I only found this out later. At this point he was

simply a guy on Facebook who wanted to meet up and I didn't see why not. There was something familiar about him and he was coming to meet me with my old friend Emma. But I didn't expect anything to happen.

The Friday of the gig arrived. I finished up my radio show and drove to Donegal. My friend Pip was meeting me there. I stopped in Strabane on the way to see another friend for a flying visit, still trying to be everything to everyone. I arrived at the hotel that evening with just enough time to shower, get ready and go to the club. My friend Glen, who was scheduled to deejay with me, was running late. He wasn't getting there any time soon, so I'd have to cut my socialising short and go to work. I texted Emma, saying I only had an hour. She texted back immediately saying she was in the pub.

Frank came out to meet me – he winked and my stomach fell to the ground.

What the hell?

It was like being hit with a thunderbolt – I had never felt anything like it. After some friendly chatting I went to work and when I saw him next he was in the club. He hung around the DJ box and I convinced myself it was Pip that he wanted, so I encouraged them both and felt stupid that I'd allowed myself to think there was anything there. Glen arrived with another friend, Bunny, so named because he never shut up. We were all staying in the one hotel room, so it was 'Party Central' back at mine, as always. Frank came back and so did his friends and we all drank, laughed and partied. Slowly, one by one, people left and then Frank got up and announced he was off.

'I've a taxi on the way.'

It seemed that I blinked and he was gone. I was gutted. Why was I feeling this way? Why did I feel so drawn to this guy? The rest of us continued to drink and party. After a while I got brave and texted him:

Cant believe I didn't get a birthday kiss.

Are you serious?

Yes, come on back?

I was feeling very brave. Things were quietening down in the room. Glen and Bunny were passed out on one of the double beds and Pip was asleep on the ironing board – a pretty standard sight, for me, to see bodies draped around my room.

Im on the way.

He was coming back. I felt a rush of adrenaline. I had decided to do something about this guy and I felt like I'd won on a slot machine. Then I remembered that I'd asked him for a kiss. What was I going to do?

The usual panic didn't arrive because the braver me was in control and the desire I felt for this guy was peaking. I went downstairs to wait for him at reception. When he walked into reception, we moved towards each other and kissed.

It seemed like Fate meant for us to be together.

I had long thought of affection and acceptance as being measured on what I could do for someone. This was something Frank couldn't understand. In the early weeks of the relationship he kept asking why I was trying to woo him with such grand gestures, like taking him to top restaurants and bars, staying in top hotels. He said he saw vulnerability in me that made him want to protect me.

He was in the army and, before he met me, had put in for a transfer to Athlone and hoped to go back to Donegal eventually. He met me the month he was due to transfer and he ended up pulling the plug on the move. He stayed in Dublin. This man I barely knew had chosen me. I couldn't get enough of him. We spent every moment together. He was like a drug to me, everything I'd always wanted and craved. *This is what love is*, I told myself. *This is it*. How did I know this? I knew it because he told me he loved me, and if he loved me, that meant that I needed him. No one had ever properly loved me before.

I asked Frank to move in with me after three weeks of being together. I had only moved into my two-bedroom townhouse in Stoneybatter that February and here I was in May with a guy I'd only met, asking him to move in with me. We had been in Ollie's apartment, singing and playing guitar the night I asked him. Frank had said he was thinking of moving out of the army barracks and wouldn't mind being city centre-based. I acted on impulse, as always.

'Move in with me.'

I remember the guys all stared at me, as if to say, 'What on earth are you doing?', but then they shrugged it off. They were used to me doing things in the extreme and I think, deep down, they believed that once I'd sobered up I'd change my tune.

When I woke the following morning I had two texts from Frank:

> Its ok I know you didn't mean what you said last night lol

And:

> Did you mean what you said last night?

I scratched my head. What did I say last night? Then it came rushing back. Sitting on his knee as he sang along and Ollie played the guitar. The impulsive offer. There were no feelings of panic or regret. I just thought, *Feck it. What can go wrong?*

And that was how I ran my life. Make the choices and deal with the consequences afterwards.

It was only after moving in with me that Frank saw how unpredictable and extreme my mood changes could be. I've asked him numerous times over the last few years: 'Why did you stay?'

'Because I loved you, I am in love with you.'

That's always his answer, even though he doesn't want anything from me. Well, nothing material, just my love.

This was unfamiliar territory. I looked at this gorgeous man who I'd already placed on a high pedestal and it wasn't long before my thoughts darkened. I began to wonder why he would stay with me. Surely everyone he looked at and met would want him? It was only a matter of time before he realised that I was ugly and horrible. As soon as he saw this he'd leave me. These thoughts – the process of beating myself up – were so deeply embedded in me that even when a sequence of good things happened I didn't allow them to sink in. I didn't enjoy that feeling. Instead I let my inner voice roar. *He can't want nothing! Maybe he just won't tell me what it is that he wants? I'm going to have to find out myself. What if I can't find out what he wants? That's it, he's going to leave me!*

All the negative thoughts would overwhelm me and, most times, leave me in tears, devastated.

Frank would walk in on me.

'What's wrong? Why are you crying?'

'You're going to leave me.'

This only succeeded in confusing Frank.

'What? Where did this come from?'

I had managed to go through all the potential scenarios and settled on the most negative possibility. I had decided on what the end scene would be and reacted as if it were a certainty. This is how my mind works. And it usually ends with me sobbing because of something that might happen, never thinking that it might not. Any torture committed on me could never be more severe than the suffering that my mind inflicts on me on a daily basis.

What if he meets someone else?

Why would he stay with you?

You're not good enough!

And so, even though he was everything I'd ever wanted, I began to push him away at every opportunity. I broke up with him twice in the first few months. We didn't actually part company, but it was as if I said the words to see if he'd leave. In some twisted way I was trying to protect myself, I realise now, each time thinking that if I pushed a little more I'd save myself from being devastated down the road. In my head it was inevitable he would leave me for someone else.

When we had been dating for about a year Frank was stationed in Lebanon with the Irish Defence Forces. I had never had a long-distance relationship before, so my anxiety levels were high and the BPD was still bubbling away undiagnosed. I would imagine negative things about him and then would cry to him as if he had actually done whatever my mind conjured. I was mentally fragile and unmedicated. In fact, I had been out of the care of the mental health services for a few years at that stage. My last contact with the mental health services had been in 2008, a year after my father's death, when I had walked out of the hospital after deciding I didn't need to be there. As was my usual routine, I had taken the anti-depressants I had been prescribed for a few months, felt better and stopped the medication without seeking any medical advice.

Frank said he always put my highs and lows down to the fact that I struggled with two very large personalities. The bubbly, confident work me and the fragile, mentally unstable me. He only learned over his deployment that there were more than two identities that I swung between, that there were in fact numerous versions of Eimear and Nikki.

I had gone so long and so far down that road of tweaking and changing to be whatever person I thought I needed to be that I honestly did not know who I really was any more. It got to the point, around this time, where I felt everyone I met was going to take away what was important in my life. For example, I used to think that someone would take my career away from me, so I lived my work life always looking over my shoulder. I was also afraid that I would lose my relationship with Frank, by far the most important part of my life. I used to think that everyone was just waiting to steal him away from me.

At one point Frank had to come home from his mission as I had been self-harming to an alarming rate and my GP had sent me to see a psychologist privately on Dame Street. After two sessions the psychologist suggested that Frank come home, as he feared that I might try to take my life again. Frank returned for a week, made sure I was connected with services and then went back to Lebanon.

I was heartbroken at his leaving and yet it was me who pushed him to go back and finish his mission.

He made another two-week trip home midway through his Lebanon tour when he returned home for his father's sixtieth birthday. He found me black and blue with a bad gash over my right eye, as I had fallen from the window ledge while hanging curtains. I had ended up being rushed to hospital after the incident, which, in a black humour sort of way, I found funny. After all, I was being rushed to hospital in an ambulance for a complete accident, whereas the times that I really needed medical intervention, such as when I'd sliced my thigh open,

I had either self-treated or driven myself to the hospital. It turned out I was badly bruised and had haematomas all down the left- and right-hand sides of my body. My eye was swollen and black, with the lids glued together.

I was ugly.

I was a piece of shit.

Why would anyone choose me?

30

BUTTERFLIES IN MY TUMMY

Not every disability is visible.

www.HealthyPlace.com

The community that you enter when having a baby is a strange one. The first time I experienced it was January 2013. By this stage Frank and I were on the move – this time to Castleknock, to a beautiful new house. The reason we were moving was that the Stoneybatter house was becoming cramped and we had also been talking about trying for a baby.

One morning, in the middle of the whole moving process, I started having a bad dose of cramping and then realised I was a few days late for my period.

I couldn't be, could I?

I'd been told by doctors that conceiving would be difficult for me because of my earlier anorexia and also because I had an ongoing case of Polycystic Ovary Syndrome, so I dismissed the idea completely. But as the day went on a tiny hope started to grow and eventually I realised I had to know one way or the other. A few hours later I returned from Boots laden with five pregnancy tests. I couldn't get this wrong. I used the first test. After a few minutes the digital screen on the test displayed:

PREGNANT – 3–4 weeks

What? I looked at it again in disbelief.

PREGNANT – 3–4 weeks

It was there in all its digital glory. I was pregnant. I went into the bedroom to Frank.

'Are you awake? I'm pregnant!'

'Well, I'm awake now,' he said. He sat up, looking as alarmed as I felt.

We went to the doctor and had it all confirmed. I was, in fact, pregnant. 'Infertile Irene' (a name I'd given myself) was pregnant. I didn't know what to do. The doctor just told me to go home, mind myself and get on a good multivitamin with folic acid.

I felt empty in the days that followed. I wondered if there was a buzz, a flutter you were meant to feel when pregnant. I didn't feel it. I probably spent too much time thinking about how I should be feeling instead of just rolling with it.

We spent the last week in January packing the boxes for our move to the new house. We moved in on 1 February and on the same day I started to bleed.

I lost the pregnancy. I'll never know what caused the

miscarriage, but the grief I felt that day – thinking about the life I'd never meet – was crippling. I realised that I desperately wanted a baby. I'll never forget the looks of sympathy and pity showered on me. I came out of A&E into Frank's arms, sobbing.

'The baby's gone. I'm not pregnant anymore.'

Frank went into protection mode, swooping in to make things better.

After the miscarriage, I was sent home and continued to unpack our belongings. I felt so down, so sad, so useless. I don't know if men truly know the effect a miscarriage can have on a woman. You feel unbelievable disappointment. The one thing we were put on this planet for at the start of human evolution was to procreate, and then you can't – your body lets you down.

Frank and I decided to try again. I obsessed about the idea of having a life grow inside me. I became focused on my ovulation patterns and even downloaded a fertility calculator app to my phone. I found myself being drawn to mothers and babies everywhere. They looked so happy. I convinced myself that this was how I could leave behind my emotional turmoil – I could shower a little life with every ounce of love I had.

After two months of trying I felt different. I can't even explain what the difference was but it was the day my period was due and I didn't have any of the normal pre-period cramping.

What the hell?

I ran out to the chemist and bought two pregnancy tests.

PREGNANT 1–2 weeks

My heart stopped. I was afraid to move. It took completing another three tests and a doctor's confirmation to convince me that I was pregnant again.

I was scared out of my wits. My body had let me down before, after all, so what if it did again? Could I go through the pain of losing another pregnancy? Physically and emotionally it was so tough. I began to hone in on the potential negative scenarios and convinced myself that I was going to have another miscarriage.

My doctor recommended I have an early scan, particularly as it was so soon after the miscarriage. The staff in the Rotunda Early Pregnancy Unit were amazing. They saw that I was frightened and did all they could to calm me down.

They placed the cold jelly on my belly and then we all stared at the screen. Nothing. No bells and whistles, no noise to represent a heart beating or anything like that.

'No heartbeat yet, but it all looks promising,' the doctor said.

No heartbeat and it all looks good? I was confused. I didn't realise that they could pick up a pregnancy before the heart starts beating. They showed me the sac and the fetal pole – which I had previously been unfamiliar with. I generally just thought you find out you're pregnant and the little beanie inside you simply grows into a bigger beanie with a heartbeat.

They booked me to come back in two weeks and, in the meantime, I locked myself in a glass case. I was so stressed that I began having regular panic attacks and grew fearful that any move that I made could result in the loss of the pregnancy. After what felt like ten weeks – it was only two – we went back to the EPU at the Rotunda. There were other couples with no visible bumps sitting around looking anxious. I didn't know what to feel. At that stage I had convinced myself the pregnancy wasn't there and I expected the very worst. Part of me always felt that the more I leaned towards the negative outcome, the more I was protecting and preparing myself for when it all inevitably fell apart.

My name was called. We went into a room with two doctors, a nurse and radiologist. They went through my chart as I lay down.

Cold jelly. Nothing. No sound. No booming heartbeat.

Anxiety gripped my chest. I looked to the doctor. The screen flashed blue. I didn't know what blue meant. *Oh my God, is this bad?* The downward spiral was already whizzing into overdrive.

'Congratulations guys, that's your baby's heartbeat,' one of the doctors announced.

I was confused. Why was there no audio? Sensing my confusion, they explained how small it was. I became transfixed by my baby, my bean, my child. This was happening. I suddenly felt happiness at a level I'd never even imagined. I was on a high – as most women would be getting this news – but I was also building up a grenade of emotions, ready to release if anything came in the way of my precious load and me.

My pregnancy felt like it would last nineteen months rather

than nine. I was scared stiff, given that I'd had the miscarriage so close to the start of the pregnancy last time. I was petrified that if I sat a certain way or looked left or right too swiftly my baby would be whipped away. The stress of trying to preserve the pregnancy – even at that early stage – was immense.

I attended prenatal classes at the hospital full of other expectant mothers. I felt like I belonged in this community. I fitted in. I had a bump; everyone had bumps. I felt like I'd just been given the golden key to a privileged society and it felt awesome. During my pregnancy yoga, when most women would be snoring at the end, I'd be looking around at all the other mums and their bumps trying to guess their due dates.

I developed pelvic girdle pain (PGP) as the pregnancy progressed, which meant frequent appointments with the physiotherapist. I looked forward to my hospital appointments, however, and tried to imagine life after my baby came along.

At the same time, I was walking on broken glass, afraid to do anything that could potentially harm the baby. I even stopped drinking my beloved tea. I became obsessed with googling every potential symptom for a miscarriage. My erratic moods and behaviours were heightened with the surge of hormones, so I was constantly snappy and going from big highs to big lows. One minute I felt I was having the best pregnancy ever, and the next I would become convinced that my baby was dead. No happy medium, no calm flow of feelings – just massive highs and lows.

In a weird kind of way, when I'm medicated and calm, I sometimes miss the mood swings. Well, not the swings themselves – God, they were chaos – but I do miss the adrenaline that they produced. It was like a fix for me, a craving. I didn't seek out the feeling but when it came I couldn't let it go. Once I began to build my own family, though, and saw how much they could be hurt, I fought hard against the desire for this feeling. I had to keep them safe – safe from me.

31

CHRISTMAS MIRACLE

It takes ten times more time and effort to put yourself back together as it does to pull yourself apart.

Suzanne Collins, *The Hunger Games: Mockingjay*

I meticulously planned the birth with Frank. I wanted it to be as natural as possible. There would be no epidural and I had looked into using transcutaneous electrical nerve stimulation (TENS), a method of pain relief involving the use of a mild electrical current. However, I was deluded to ever think you can properly plan giving birth. I've since learned that the baby will come the way baby wants to and that's that.

I was due on 12 December and, with it being so close to Christmas, I was getting excited. I was going to have a baby for Christmas. I managed to maintain this excitement even though I had gained three stone and clearly looked pregnant. I know people say that you glow when you're pregnant, but it's a cop out. I was three stone heavier, had fluid building up in my face and neck; I looked severely bloated and had kankles (knees that meet ankles) that were the size of my waist. I was a big mamma.

I remember that I hadn't seen two of our close friends, Conor and Niall, for a few months, what with me locking myself away from the world during my pregnancy. Frank and I met them for food one evening to wish them a happy Christmas. I'll never forget walking in and the way Niall appeared to look at me. I lip-read him saying, 'Holy God, she's huge' and I felt like I wanted to fade away like a ghost before reaching their table.

I felt self-conscious as we ate our meal and had the constant need to rub my belly so everyone knew I actually was pregnant and not just weighty. That's something I regret. I never properly enjoyed my pregnancy because – as well as living in a constant fear that I would lose the baby – I hated how the pregnancy made me so fat. There were girls in work constantly having babies and they were 'only bump', so still kept their figures. Soon after birth they were back down to pre-pregnancy size and looked like proper yummy mummies.

Putting myself in a glass case for my pregnancy meant I had stopped drinking caffeine, chamomile tea and sodas, and eating meat (unless it was burnt), as well as certain fruits. The list went on. Anything I googled that said 'may harm during pregnancy' – even if it was a one-off study from 1990 – I added to the list. I also cut out exercise for fear of hurting the baby. I basically hibernated for my pregnancy. I got annoyed at people on the street who smoked in my vicinity, believing they would harm my baby in some way with their streams of poison. I was highly strung. Every move was filled with anxiety. I couldn't relax. I lost count of the amount of times I visited my GP or ended up in

A&E at the Rotunda convinced that my baby was dead. You are meant to enjoy your pregnancy, let it be a mostly happy time. Instead I was fearful for most of the entire nine months.

When it came close to the due date for my baby, the midwife scheduled me to come in for a sweep, which is a procedure whereby the midwife will insert a finger into the opening of your cervix and then gently but firmly move her finger around. This action should separate the membranes of the amniotic sac surrounding your baby from your cervix and induce labour. (I know, too much information!) The reason for the sweep is to encourage labour to start naturally.

The sweep definitely started something as I felt period-like cramps for a day or two afterwards. Then the cramping stopped. The following week, when I was being checked again, my baby wasn't moving. They brought me to A&E and put me on a movement monitor for the baby and ran a heart trace. I was on my own, as Frank was on a course for work. I was petrified that something was wrong with my baby. I remembered my niece, Hollie, and how she'd been stillborn. The doctor came in and told me to drink a sugary drink. After a bottle of Lucozade, she read the results.

'She's there alright, you can see her moving. She was just a bit sluggish.'

'What?' I asked. '*She's* there alright?'

'Don't you know what you're having?' she asked.

'No, we wanted it to be a surprise.'

Her face fell. 'Oh well, I couldn't see properly. The baby was turned away from the camera.'

Even though she denied knowing for sure, it was then that I knew I was having a little girl. All my childhood feelings washed up again in my mind. I wanted her to have everything I never had and I wanted to become the protective figure that I had always craved.

I was given another sweep and sent home.

That weekend I was having twinges and felt very uncomfortable. I couldn't settle, either in a seated position or when I was lying down. The only relief I got was sitting on the toilet. I presumed this was the start of things and grew petrified. I couldn't get warm enough. I had leggings, bootie slippers, fluffy socks, my jumper and Frank's hoodie on but still couldn't get comfortable or warm. I shivered incessantly.

The pain was frightening me now. I had never felt a pain like it and this was a pain over which I had no control. This pain was controlling me.

I called the midwife; she said it sounded like things were starting, but that there was a long road to go. I was now 40+2 (two days overdue for the men). Frank was working and had told me to call him if anything got more painful or if my waters broke. I hopped into the bath and felt ripples in my stomach. It felt like indigestion, but of a sort that I had never experienced before. Maybe that was all it was. Maybe I just needed to sit on the toilet for a while – so I did, for three hours, with blessed relief, until Frank came home. I don't know why that particular position gave me such relief but I certainly wasn't questioning anything at that point.

As my waters hadn't broken and it was nearing Christmas

week, my consultant offered me an induction on St Stephen's Day. I took it and went back home with mild cramping. I felt dizzy and unwell so lay down and tried to sleep. I was exhausted and yet I couldn't close my eyes for too long because when I did I imagined the horror of the baby dying. Every negative possibility ran through my head until I actually made myself sick. I fell asleep that night, curled into a ball, my arms wrapped around my bump, willing her to be okay.

When I woke early the next morning, 16 December, I could see I had some leakage (it's not nice whatever way I write it, but 'leakage' won over the other suitable words). I rang Frank in work and asked him to come home and bring me to the hospital. He thought it would be too early, as I wasn't getting any contractions. But I was catastrophising; I felt I was going to lose my baby and die, so I convinced him to drive me to A&E.

'You're definitely not in labour yet,' he said.

If this isn't labour, then what am I in for when it's the real thing?

All I felt was panic and pain.

Due to the fact I was so highly strung about the labour, the doctor admitted me to the prenatal ward for rest and some gas. I think I went through two canisters of gas that night, trying to keep the pain from rearing its head at all. They booked me in for an induction the following morning. Frank went home and returned at 8 a.m.

I was brought down to the labour ward and suddenly it all felt real. One way or another I was having a baby today.

The least twinge sent me into a panic. I had my own room and my own appointed midwife for the labour and she was our saving grace. Frank tried to soothe me too. I know, looking back, that my anxiety must have been driving him through the roof. The doctors came around and the first thing they did was break my waters. I couldn't believe the amount of water that was flowing from me. It seemed relentless. (I'm sorry for being graphic here but there is no pleasant way of realistically describing giving birth.)

The doctors came back shortly after to check on me. I heard one of them say, 'The baby has meconium in the waters.'

This meant the baby had pooped slightly and there was a risk of it being fatal if it blocked the baby's airways. I shared with the doctors the fact that my niece had died in childbirth and the first sign that she was in distress had been meconium in the waters. They saw my complete panic and decided to start me on the drip that would stimulate contractions.

The contractions came slowly at first, but steadily gained in speed and intensity. I panicked. I just wanted someone to get the baby out and to know it was okay. I didn't want to feel this pain any more. The contractions were starting to be painful and the gas wasn't doing anything for me. Fluid continued to flow and yet I remained only two centimetres dilated.

After seven hours in labour, I folded and asked for the epidural. I couldn't do this any more. Even my high threshold for pain had been broken and I was exhausted with worry, panic and stress. The anaesthesiologist was called. He twice attempted and failed to insert the epidural. (The needle needs to be placed in a very precise area at the base of your spine, which by the way, hurts like hell!) The third attempt was successful and it quickly took effect. I had a couple of pain-free hours, but was still only four centimetres dilated.

This baby was going nowhere.

At 8 p.m. that evening the doctor came to check on me again. The epidural had worn off and they couldn't give me any more. The false contractions from the induction were coming hard and fast. I had never before felt pain like it. The midwife and consultant could see the distress I was in and Frank just looked helpless. A decision was made to bring me to theatre for a Caesarean section as my blood pressure was lowering. Baby was fine, mama not so much.

The consultant explained to Frank that they would hit the emergency bell and that things would happen very quickly but not to worry. When the bell went everything spun above me as I was rushed by a team down to theatre. The excruciating pain had me growling and roaring at this stage.

We got to theatre and the anaesthesiologist and Frank were by my side. I was administered a full spinal block, the screen was placed so we didn't see the Caesarean take place. I felt a slight tugging, which Frank told me after was my body being jerked as the surgeon pulled Farah from my womb. Then silence. Frank looked at me, his face full of anticipation. I was groggy and shivering.

Then that cry, the one when you know everything is going to be okay.

After the relief came shock. I was wrapped up as my body

went into complete shock. Frank was pushed out while they sewed me up. I didn't see our baby. I knew it was a girl and the nurses told me she was doing well.

I drifted off and woke a little while later in post-op with Frank there and our baby, Farah, lying beside me in her crib. The nurse gave me some water. I was incredibly thirsty after everything. She asked me if I'd like to feed my daughter. Due to the Caesarean and the fact that I'd been administered morphine I wasn't going to be able to breastfeed, and, to be honest, I wouldn't have had the energy to right then, but they'd made up a bottle for her. She took it and started guzzling straight away.

Frank later told me that as soon as he was pushed out of the theatre and into the side room, he called his mum and broke down crying, as he had been left with this tiny bundle while his fiancée was in shock in theatre. (Apparently with Caesareans it can take the mind a few minutes to catch up with the fact that you've had major surgery and that is why you can go into shock.) As they were stitching me back up and stabilising me, the nurses checked our baby girl over and cut the cord. Then she'd been swaddled and given to Frank.

The time in post-op was busy with nurses in and out checking on me and the phone constantly pressed to my ear, speaking to the in-laws, my brother, my sister, my mother, my friends. I was exhausted. Labour from start to finish had lasted for three days.

Around 10.30 p.m. my little girl and I were wheeled up to the post-labour ward. A doctor came to see me and said that I had passed on a virus called Group B Strep to our baby, so she'd need to go to the natal ward for antibiotics twice a day for three days. He also reassured me that the virus was nothing serious. Only a few babies who are exposed to GBS actually become infected, but if they do it can be very serious and in severe cases lead to death, so to be on the safe side they administer antibiotics just in case. Farah was absolutely fine.

The women on the ward were all lovely, all had their own stories and all had been through Caesareans. We chatted, cooed over each other's babies and drank lots of tea. The tea and toast I had post-birth were the tastiest I've ever had. The legend that labour ward toast is divine is true!

I floated through the next few days. Morphine allowed me to get up and walk around without feeling intense pain. Frank's parents were coming down to stay with us for Christmas and give us a hand. I loved his parents and was looking forward to having them stay. I was discharged the day before Christmas Eve, and Frank and his dad picked up me and Farah from the Rotunda.

I was glad to be going, but a little panicked that my support network of midwives and doctors were being left behind. This was it, I realised. There was no going back now.

32

I DON'T KNOW HOW TO BE A MUM

From the moment she was born … I felt an instant, radical, unconditional love that redefined love.

Bryan Cranston, *A Life in Parts*

I remember the fear I felt in those early days, looking at this little mite in her rock-a-tot and fluffy white snowsuit. She relied on me for everything, even though I couldn't even rely on me. How on earth was this going to work? I had the third-day baby blues in hospital but it was minor compared to what lay ahead.

That first day when we arrived home, Mary (Frank's mum), had the dinner and fire on. The house was toasty, and I remember she gave me a big welcoming hug and smile. Farah's Moses basket was dressed and waiting in the sitting room. I went to have a shower. Afterwards, I sat down on the bed and started sobbing. I was sore, I was never going to make a good mother and I just wanted to go to sleep. Mary walked in on me and put her arms around me. I just couldn't hold back the tears.

I was on morphine for a week after giving birth and with Frank's parents at the helm I took the opportunity to sleep. As everyone says, it becomes precious once a baby comes along. I slept days and nights. Even Christmas Day I woke in the morning and went back to sleep. I was woken up for dinner. I came downstairs to the sound of Christmas music and the odour of a Christmas dinner that smelled delicious. I, however, had no appetite. I sat at the kitchen table and didn't want to be there.

What is wrong with you?

Mary had placed Farah in her Moses basket in the adjacent living room while we ate. The nearby open fire warmed her. She was fast asleep and more than in our eye-line and earshot, but this wasn't enough for me. I broke into a sweat. 'She's going to burn alive.' This despite the fact that a fireguard was up and we were in the next room.

Everyone looked at me – I was panic-stricken. If I didn't move my baby right now from the living room I was certain she'd die. I burst into tears, so Mary went in and had her Christmas dinner on her lap, sitting beside Farah's crib. I wanted to sleep and so after managing a few forkfuls of ham I went back to bed.

The public health nurse called to the house and I spoke to her about how I was feeling. She was satisfied that Farah was doing well and that I was simply having the baby blues as well as a slight withdrawal from the morphine.

The withdrawals were difficult. I remember lying in bed at one point, hallucinating that there was a man standing over my bed. I was soaked in sweat. My howl was so loud it sent Frank and his dad running to my side. I sat up shivering and crying. I constantly felt like I wanted to go to sleep and never wake up. The tiredness was so overwhelming.

That same day I heard a shrill cry and tuned in to the conversation below me.

'Mum, she won't wind for me,' I heard Frank say.

'She's caught up, the poor pet. Give her here.'

Cries again. Farah sounded like she was in pain. Was my baby in pain? She needed her mother. She needed me. I ran downstairs and walked into the living room. I screeched 'Give me my baby!' and snatched her from Mary's arms and brought her up to bed with me. When I look back, I see that I acted appallingly but I know now that I didn't act with sanity, as that was the start of what was going to be a long battle with post-natal depression.

33

POST-NATAL DISTRESS

It takes a strong person to say sorry,
And an even stronger person to forgive.

Vanessa Guzman

Having a new baby is daunting, especially when it's your first. I put myself under such immense pressure to be 100 per cent perfect at everything. I felt anything below 100 per cent was terrible. The lack of sleep and overdrive of hormones that went with being a new mum, of course, did not allow for me to be 'Supermum'. I was fighting a losing battle.

It didn't help that I struggled to bond with Farah immediately. When I looked at her I knew that I loved her, but I also felt that she was hard work. You're not meant to think your own child is hard work, are you? After three weeks the public health nurse started noticing the baby blues were increasing instead of dissipating. She referred me to a post-natal support group and suggested that I attend for emotional support. I hated groups, I hated opening up to strangers and yet, deep down, I felt this was what I needed. If I went to this course I'd be fixed and could then become the best mother ever.

The next course placement wasn't until Farah was eight weeks old. So I sat back and tried to get on with things in the meantime. The problem was that things seemed to be unravelling. I was falling into a deeper spiral of self-hatred and the belief that I was unable to be a mum of any kind grew stronger. At this time, Frank had also applied to serve overseas with the defence forces and so we braced ourselves for what lay ahead.

The post-natal course was a lifeline for the time that I attended. It became clear, even to me, that I was not a well bunny. I was down low and struggling to stand. I was living in a constant state of fear and anxiety, and so I found it difficult to just relax and enjoy being a mother. I expected big things, and if I didn't perform to the impossible standards that I had set for myself, I proceeded to punish myself.

Over the eight weeks of the course, it became clear to the public health nurse and psychologist running the course that I wasn't getting any better and I wasn't getting the same benefit from sharing as some of the other women. I won't lie, it was a support knowing that others were feeling the struggle too, but they weren't horrible, lowlife mums like me. I couldn't even respect myself. I had started cutting myself again. Small cuts that I could hide, but enough that they would give me the release I desired.

Things took a turn for the worse when Frank found out at the start of May that he was being sent to Syria for six months. I already felt exhausted, as I'd not stopped since the day Farah was born. My daughter and I went everywhere, did everything together and yet I felt we didn't really have a strong bond created from spending 'real' time together. Without even noticing it, I decided I was becoming everything I feared – a terrible mother. I worried that I wasn't feeling the unbreakable connection I should have with my daughter and was convinced that I wasn't giving her enough affection. And now I was going to lose the one person who was always there for me.

I started to fall apart again. The post-natal support group had ended by this time and I was referred to see the mental health team in Roselawn Health Clinic in Blanchardstown. I was diagnosed officially with post-natal depression (PND) and started on a high dose of anti-depressants. These helped regulate things for a while, but the extreme mood swings and highs and lows did reappear. I tried putting on another mask, pretending I could cope when Frank went overseas. But just before he was due to start an intensive training plan in preparation for Syria, I broke. I took a handful of Diazepam and passed out. Frank was frantic with worry. He called my doctor and was advised that I should start to attend a day hospital in Blanchardstown. This is a facility owned and run by the HSE mental health services that provides psychological support and monitoring, but leaves its patients their independence, allowing them to go home in the evening.

I was experiencing huge emotional swings at the time and, looking back, I can see that it was the emotionally unstable part of the BPD really coming to the surface, although of course we didn't know it then. To be honest, I had never even heard of BPD at the time.

34

ABANDONMENT

You can't force love, I realized. It's there or it isn't. If it's not there, you've got to be able to admit it. If it is there, you've got to do whatever it takes to protect the ones you love.

Richelle Mead, *Frostbite*

That summer was tough. My focus was on getting strong, or at least pretending to get strong, in time for Frank's departure. Frank himself was away in Athlone a lot of the time, training, and I was back to work, juggling a five-day week with crèche drops and pick-ups. I was living like a single mother and yet my partner was out there. He just couldn't be with me. He came home as often as he could, even making the six-hour round-trip in the car some days just so he could see for himself that his fiancée and daughter were okay. I missed him so much and yet I tried to turn off my emotions and become somewhat detached to prepare myself for his deployment. I had met a lot of army WAGS over the years and some loved the army life while others just about managed. I was definitely part of the latter group. I couldn't understand when some of the wives would say, 'It's great. You get time to yourself and money to treat yourself when he sends it home.'

I didn't want to treat myself; I wanted my fiancé to be there. I wanted him to hold me and protect me and tell me everything was going to be okay.

A multidisciplinary team in the mental health services saw me as Frank's deployment date to Syria approached. I had a nurse who called to the house and an occupational therapist who worked through mindfulness and coping strategies with me. My psychologist helped me to make sense of what was happening and showed me how to move forward, as did my consultant, who sat at the helm of all my treatment.

I was also medicated during this time. A mood stabiliser was added to my usual course of anti-depressants, as my mood swings had become so prominent we couldn't ignore them. I would have three to four appointments a week with them through the day hospital. They were aware of all my issues, from Frank leaving, to the fact that my depression and anxiety were at very acute levels. My body image had become a target again and I was cutting myself regularly to release the anger I felt towards myself. I was kept under a close eye as, soon enough, the time came to say goodbye.

Frank was scared senseless. He didn't want to leave us and yet he couldn't afford not to go. The money from overseas deployment was good and with no savings we had no choice.

I drove him to the airbase in the last week of September. He was flying out of Baldonnel Aerodrome. I drove to the entrance with our nine-month-old, who was oblivious to what was happening as she slept in the back of a car I had borrowed from Toyota. (The car manufacturers are great at loaning some of their models in return for social media mentions.) As we had no car ourselves, they had kindly loaned me one for the weeks before and after Frank's deployment to make life a bit easier for me.

The last overseas trip had been hell for us both, but when he had been deployed to Lebanon things were different. We hadn't had a child together and I hadn't been responsible for anyone but myself. Farah was nine months old now and was changing every day. I was being treated for acute PND and a mood disorder. We had no family close by to help and, because of my inability to retain close friends, we had very few supportive people living around us.

Frank's parents were amazing around this time. They would come visit as often as possible and having them come and stay with me meant that I felt part of Frank's life again.

Frank had his birthday soon after landing in Syria. This upset me, as I wanted to be the one getting him cake. I wanted to be the one spoiling him. Instead he was a six-hour flight away, in a war-torn country with a bunch of strangers, most of whom I'd never met. I looked at the photos of him on Facebook being presented with his cake and having a few beers as he sat around a long table and I felt deflated. In my head it seemed like there he was having the time of his life, while I was left behind struggling to keep my head above water and getting tired of all the costume changes. Of course that wasn't the case at all.

Frank's trip to Syria meant that he missed Farah's first

Halloween, first birthday, first Christmas, first St Patrick's Day and first Easter. Both of us felt every milestone. He was upset to be missing them and I was finding it tough to keep up the façade that I was actually coping in his absence.

Farah's birthday was probably one of the hardest moments for me during this period, made worse by the fact that it was so close to Christmas. I had decided to stay at home on my own with her. I bought a small ham in Dunnes Stores and a turkey crown. It would be enough for a few days. Then I sat in my pyjamas for two days consumed by the idea that it was somehow my fault that Frank wasn't there. This wasn't a logical thought, but I still managed to blame myself.

Farah had a lovely Christmas. She was fascinated by the lights on the tree and all the presents. She knew something was going on but wasn't quite sure what it was. We had purchased her a mini ball-pool, which she was so excited about, as well as jigsaws and learning toys. She was such a good baby. She was happy to spend time online, looking at Daddy as we spoke on Skype and giving him lots of smiles, and then she would do the same thing all over again with her grandparents in Donegal.

In contrast Christmas brought me low. I was 100 per cent isolated. There was no one to look after me. I was back to cooking dinner for one on Christmas Day. The floodgates were opening. The negativity of that time was leading to what would become the biggest rollercoaster of my life.

Going back to work after Christmas, everyone looked refreshed, happy, glowing. After dropping Farah to the crèche, I went in in my usual attire of leggings and a long top to cover my massive bum. Everyone was full of stories about their nights out over Christmas, their family arguments and all the presents they'd received. It was hard to be surrounded by so much positivity when I felt so bad.

Then, just when I thought things couldn't become any more difficult, I was proven wrong. My landlord contacted me to say that at the end of the term of our lease – which was in a few weeks' time – he was selling up. So we had to get out.

I was panic-stricken. My husband was overseas, I didn't have a car and I had no one to help me. I called Frank in tears, catastrophising again. 'We are going to be homeless!'

As usual, Frank stepped up. He organised for Conor, his best friend and Farah's godfather, to help me view houses and also to help me move. We were lucky in that we found a house quite quickly in the same postal code. It was over budget but we had no choice. I moved us in with help from Conor and from Claire (Farah's babysitter, who had become a close friend). The move took us three days but we got there.

After the stress of moving house, I began trying hard to banish the negative, critical voice that was growing and starting to overpower me again. I couldn't tell Frank about it – I didn't want to worry him. I'd done that enough in the past. So I told him that the doctors were delighted with me and had suggested that I cut down on my medication. They never said this. I withdrew from my weekly psychology appointments and was never home when my nurse called to the house. I came off my medication, cold turkey.

With BPD you can convince yourself at times that if you

take the focus off your mental instability, then it will go away – you fool yourself and other people that everything is okay. This is a pattern that I have found myself repeating time and again.

On this occasion I convinced myself I would be in control of my life by the time Frank came home and he would see how strong I had become. I truly believed that I could do it but, of course, it wasn't sustainable long-term.

35

SWEEPING ME UNDER THE CARPET

There is a delicate balance of putting yourself last and not being a doormat and thinking of yourself first and not coming off as selfish, arrogant or bossy. We spend the majority of our lives attempting to perfect this balance.

Cindy L. Teachey

One bright spot for me at this time was that Frank had told me he wanted to get married when he returned from Syria. We had got engaged when he returned from his previous tour of duty in Lebanon. He had whisked me to Lough Eske Castle in Co. Donegal, telling me that we were having a night away. Before dinner that evening he led me to the tower. It was lit up with candles all along the stairs and at the top he set out a picnic and dropped to one knee. It was the most romantic thing that ever happened to me.

Now we were planning for the big day and I was over the moon. I had fun planning the wedding. At first, I dreamed of big budgets. Everything felt more real, however, when our budget was set at a realistic level. We agreed, for example, that we would have a small venue. After checking out multiple venues we decided on The Angler's Rest, a restaurant and wedding venue in Castleknock, Co. Dublin. It was close to where we lived, yet nestled in the countryside setting of the Strawberry Beds by the canal. We could have the ceremony there too, and keep everyone in the one area. It seemed perfect.

As the weeks passed, however, I kept worrying about how people would get there. I didn't want to upset anyone.

Eventually I called Frank.

'The wedding is off,' I declared.

'What? Why?'

(The extreme mood swings had returned at this point, given that I was off my meds, but with Frank being away, I was managing to hide them from him.)

I listed the reasons why I felt the wedding should be called off. I couldn't lose weight, I couldn't afford a proper wedding dress (I'd bought two for less than €30 which had no shape), and we couldn't afford The Angler's Rest.

I was catastrophising, of course, but Frank could hear the panic in my voice and so he agreed that maybe we should wait.

We were gutted but I was determined to rebook ASAP. So I did – for the day after the initial date. Seriously! I was acting impulsively and irrationally. I was sitting on the top of my wall of sanity and I was about to fall over the other side. For the following date, we called a friend of ours, Niall, who owns a bar/restaurant in the city centre called Alfies. We put the idea to him and he loved it. So we had a new venue. Thankfully, we were both so happy with our choice in the end.

Frank returned from Syria a week before we were due to marry. It was strange, at first, seeing him. He seemed to come back a very different man – I think the distance of time and geography had made him unfamiliar to me, like I was meeting him for the first time. He had lost a lot of weight and inside I questioned whether or not he still loved me.

Farah was strange with him in the airport, even though they had spoken often on Skype. I think her fear may have had more to do with him being outside the computer screen. I could nearly hear her think, 'Ehhhh, how did you get out of my computer?' After about ten minutes, though, she put her arms out to him and I knew then everything would be okay.

Given that the return was so close to the wedding, Frank had a million things to do, such as having his stag, getting suits for him, his best man Conor and his father. All these distractions meant that Frank didn't see how much my mental stability was failing.

For our wedding day we had decided to keep it small and not to invite extended family, as we only wanted the people who were part of our daily lives to be there with us and our budget was limited. I asked my friend Audrey to be my maid of honour and Dessie (Frank's dad) to give me away. He had only three boys, so this would be his first and maybe only time to lead a bride down the aisle. He was very special to me as he was the father figure I had been missing from my life since my own father died in 2007. My mother and father-in-law,

Mary and Dessie Black, had, after all, taken me in as their own daughter. His mother has often told me, 'You're the daughter we never had.'

I've been close to Frank's family from day one. When Frank moved in with me after a few weeks his mum made it clear she was glad for us. Both his parents have supported us through everything and since we had Farah they have gone above and beyond to show us that they are there for us. When I had to move house his parents were constantly on the phone to me, offering emotional support. When Frank was in Lebanon they would come and stay with me. When Frank proposed to me, his whole family were in on it, even offering to mind the dogs for us. When I miscarried his parents were there for us straight away. When I got pregnant again so soon afterwards they were supportive the whole way through. When Farah was born they came to stay for a few weeks to help us with her. I'm grateful every day for their support. Mary has been a loving, non-judgemental maternal figure, who talks to me about emotional stuff and gives me advice on mothering-related matters. Dessie is protective and has always been a huge support. This is the main reason why I asked him to give me away on our wedding day.

We had thirty-five people with us to celebrate our marriage. The ceremony was at the Dublin Registry Office. I wore a dress donated to me by a lovely lady from whom I had bought my wedding shoes on Adverts.ie. To this day I only know her as MishkaMoon. She had asked me to send a photo of my dress so she could make sure the shoes matched. They were stunning, immaculate Nine West shoes. She sold them to me for €40. When I sent her the photo she replied:

A short dress? How come?

I explained I'd bought a lace one off eBay but had been delivered a dress that basically looked like a tablecloth with a lot of bad sewing work. She said the shoes matched perfectly and she'd send them the following day. Another thing ticked off my list.

When the shoes arrived, however, the package was massive. When I opened it my jaw dropped. Inside the box were my shoes, but also a stunning tiara and a satin, boned, strapless gown with a jewel-encrusted top. I was shocked. Thank you gift cards and heart balloons were also included.

I instantly messaged her and said that I couldn't accept the dress. When she wouldn't back down I demanded that she at least allow me to pay for it. She turned that down too. She said she was moving to America and couldn't take things with her. She asked me to make a promise to her.

Anything.

When you're finished with the dress, pass it on.

I will, I promise.

I was shocked by this generous gift. I had also been lucky with Farah's flower-girl dress and managed to buy it at a cheap price on Adverts.ie. Brand new, it had just been a size too big for the girl who needed it. It fitted Farah perfectly.

My dress needed some slight adjustments, so I set about finding a tailor to do some work expanding the back and bust. I had two weeks to go. After some research I found a lovely girl, Miriam, in Co. Carlow. I called her and she said if I came down that day she'd have it to me by the end of the week. Relief. I got into the car and drove southbound to Carlow. The detailing on the dress was so beautiful that Miriam didn't want to cut into it. Instead she decided to remove the zip and create a corset-style back. This would maintain the detailing and allow for more wiggle room. I have always been grateful for the speed and dedication she showed. The finished product was stunning.

36

I DO

Even miracles take a little time.

Fairy Godmother, *Cinderella*

When the day arrived, 8 May 2015, I was so chilled out. Audrey had stayed with me the night before and I woke up to find her fast asleep beside me. I nudged her and she jumped out of bed. The hair and make-up girls were going to be arriving soon. Frank's mother and father had also stayed with me and they were up already with Farah. I wasn't nervous at all. The girl doing our hair had only been booked three days ago. She settled into doing Mary's hair, then Audrey's hair and came to me last. Simple curls with the tiara placed on top. I went last again when the make-up lady arrived. I sat on the couch with a glass of Prosecco and tweeted away on my phone. It frightened me how relaxed I was, as I'm normally so pent up.

The weather that day was awful. It rained all day; there wasn't a break for even a few minutes. It was the day a baby was found abandoned in a shopping bag at the side of a road in north Co. Dublin. That always jogs Dublin-based people's memories as to how bad the weather was that day.

A friend of Frank's from the army drove Audrey and me to the registry office. He ran his own taxi service and was one of the nicest men you could ever meet – a real gentleman. Frank's mum and dad and Farah followed behind in my car, which Frank had bought me when he returned from Syria to make getting around easier.

Dessie was beside me, proud as punch, as we walked up the aisle. It was unconventional giving me away to his son, but to hell with tradition – this went beyond that.

As I read my vows to Frank, he kept looking at me and telling me to breathe. I was choking with emotion. My jaw ached from trying not to cry. It was overwhelming, standing in front of this man – the love of my life – in the presence of our nearest and dearest, telling him exactly how he made me feel, exactly what he meant to me. I was raw and stuck to the spot – telling this man that I needed and wanted him for the rest of my life. As we held hands and everyone clapped, our friend Nella Dwyer sang one of our favourite songs, Fisher's 'I Will Love You'. Nella's voice is so pure and special.

Due to the rain, we couldn't have any outdoor photos, but the Guinness Storehouse kindly allowed us to take photos in there, which was different and a bit of craic. I remember Americans including me in their holiday snaps, and we also got some really nice ones at the top of the storehouse with Dublin sprawled out behind us.

We had an amazing wedding day. Even Farah's godmother, Bambi, had made it, despite being eight-and-a-half months pregnant. It was busy and we were on the move all day. The staff in Alfies couldn't do enough for us and after dinner and speeches were over we all retired to the top floor to chill, listen to music and chat. We invited another forty people for the afters – people who I worked with and Frank worked with, as well as friends we maybe didn't see or talk to very often but were still around. It was one of the happiest days of my life.

The next morning, waking up, it did not feel like the day after we got married. We woke up in our own bed, got up with our daughter and had breakfast. Frank's parents were still with us as they were taking Farah for a week to allow us to go on our honeymoon. We were heading to Albufeira in Portugal. We'd been there before and knew what to expect.

I'd never been away from Farah since she'd been born, so I expected this was going to be difficult. During the trip, I worried about her and felt guilty for a few days, but then the sunshine of the Algarve healed my worries and I started to relax.

On the honeymoon, my inability to handle alcohol alarmed Frank. For a girl who in the past could always manage to drink plenty, I was now wobbling after just two or three. Frank mentioned it in concern a few times and I bit back at him: 'I'm fine, I'm just not used to drinking since you've been away.' He gave up for a few days and put my merry moods down to the fact that I could let loose without the responsibility of minding Farah.

By day four of the honeymoon, we were eager to try some authentic Portuguese food. We had waited a few days to get a reservation in one of Albufeira's highest-rated local cuisine restaurants. We turned up early and went into the sports bar beside the restaurant and had a few games of pool and a few bottles of beer. We were relaxing and enjoying ourselves when a group of Northern Irish tourists joined in. They found out we were on honeymoon and ordered a bottle of Prosecco to celebrate. We were only too happy to take a glass and the glass then turned into another bottle. I felt woozy with the heat and the amount of alcohol I'd taken.

We kept to our dinner reservation and went into the restaurant hoping that we would sober up a little with some food inside us. We had spent the entire week looking forward to the piri piri chicken that was served there. The waiter came and we ordered wine. The menu came. I looked, but nothing caught my eye. I had forgotten why we had come here in the first place.

'An omelette, please,' I ordered.

'What?' Frank asked. 'What about the chicken? You can't come to a highly rated Portuguese restaurant and order an omelette.'

For some reason, though, at that very moment in time all I wanted was an omelette. There was no changing my mind. Frank was feeling the effects of a day drinking in the sun too but he kept drinking water and Coke, whereas I frequently topped up my wine glass.

I don't remember much else. Frank said the omelette arrived and I didn't want it. I then proceeded to fall asleep on the plate. The restaurant was busy and Frank decided to leave and head home. I came around in the taxi. When he told me what happened I was embarrassed.

What a stupid, ignorant mess you are.

Back at our room, I went and sat on the balcony, looking out at the night sky. Frank was sleeping soundly inside. I had been off my medication for two months at this stage (I had told Frank that the doctors said I didn't need to be on it any more). I picked up a nearby corkscrew and stabbed it into my leg. The feeling of being out of control consumed me, as did the desire to cut harder and deeper. To stop myself, I jumped up from my chair and went inside. Frank woke up and became worried about my pacing around the apartment. I made sure that he didn't see the wound I'd given myself – I'd become so used to hiding them over the years it wasn't difficult. He asked me to take a break from the drink as the mixture of heat and alcohol weren't suiting me at all. He was right, I told myself. I could go into shock and die of a heart attack.

This wasn't true, of course, but I was suddenly feeling anxious and vulnerable. Life had been so hectic for the last year: I had Farah; I developed post-natal depression, the treatment of which I failed to prioritise; there had also been Frank's deployment to Syria. I had continued spiralling down and down and down during this time.

Despite this, we did have a wonderful honeymoon. Frank organised picnics on the beach, we walked to isolated coves and inlets, in through caves with the most spectacular formations. But, looking back, everything had been so hectic in the lead-up to the wedding that it was not really surprising that this fall happened.

37

MASQUERADE MASTER

Some people don't believe in heroes
But they have never met my husband.

Loveydoveydiva.com

You can become quite the master of disguise when living with BPD. At times, Frank could tell that I was finding things really hard, but there were also times when he saw what appeared to be a very satisfied woman, when, in reality, my moods and thoughts were all over the place.

After we got home from the honeymoon, I went back to the mental health service to try to get some help. As we had moved house, I was referred to see a different consultant and a whole new team. But it was nice to know that I now had support and could give up fighting against myself. Day-to-day living can be so tough and frustrating, particularly when you are your own biggest opponent. With the new team I was medicated again and assigned a new psychologist and nurse. But because I was still being treated for post-natal depression, and my BPD remained undiagnosed, the help I was receiving was largely ineffective.

That summer of 2015 was up and down for us. I was very manic and felt that I was causing everyone pain and torture. I couldn't look people in the eyes, as I was convinced something bad would happen. The wedding and honeymoon had been my main focus over the last few months. I was without that distraction now and therefore all I could do was disappear into the darkness of my mind. The more I felt myself spiral down, the more I would push myself to appear normal. I thought that if nobody suspected that anything was wrong with me, then I would be able to convince myself too. Looking back, I know this wasn't rational, but when I was in that downward pattern of thoughts, it made perfect sense to me.

Of course the negative thoughts just grew stronger. I needed to be hurt. I needed to be punished. I was disgusting. I was worthless. I would be better off dead.

I managed to convince myself over those summer months that Frank and Farah would be better off without me. I truly believed that I was obese, ugly, hideous and unworthy. I felt like a bad mother. Farah deserved better. I even said to Frank, 'When I die make sure whoever you meet is good to Farah.'

Frank hated when I started down this path of conversation because it always ended up the same way – with me in floods of tears, shaking with fear.

I decided to do things for Frank to make him happy, so he could be away from me and spend time with people I considered more worthy of him. I bought him tickets to matches. I told him I got them for free through work, but instead spent over €200 of my own money on premium seats.

I wanted to do everything to make him feel special, as I didn't feel my love was enough.

Of course, this put me back on the path of buying gifts that I couldn't afford. I started to get into debt again and had the added pressure of hiding that. Every time a notice letter for unpaid debts came through the letterbox, I jumped, fear spearing through me, but I just couldn't stop myself.

38

I'M JOHNNY LYONS

Sports today is a smorgasbord of action and skill.

Johnny Lyons #RIP

Work was becoming a struggle. SPIN 1038 was a very youth-orientated, happy station. My friends used to call it the 'bubble-gum and rainbows' station and that's not far off. Working in SPIN was unique. I've never worked anywhere else where your colleagues become such a part of your life. This always made me feel a little uncomfortable, as I didn't like people getting too close to me.

In SPIN everyone greeted you with hugs and OMGs every time you walked in the door. It was an atmosphere where people almost sat on your knee talking to you. People were friendly, good humoured and beautiful – everything I felt I wasn't. I was an alien in the SPIN galaxy.

I was so afraid of meeting people and being rejected that I isolated myself within the workspace. After the first few months of my re-employment with the broadcaster, the CEO had to tell me to sit closer to people as, with my desk furthest up the corridor, I appeared like the Independent Republic of

Nikki. It was said with warmth and so I did move, and I'm glad I did. People relaxed around me as soon as I settled into the fold and became more approachable. In truth, SPIN provided me with years of fun and pleasant memories, but it was also the hardest place in the world for me to be when I felt low.

My body image issues have never gone away. I am never happy with how I look. I hate my body, I hate my weight, I hate my face, I hate my hair ... I could keep going on, but I'm sure you get the picture. In SPIN I worked with a female-heavy staff. The girls who worked there were – and still are – stunning. A lot were promoted from our street team and therefore were bubbly and beautiful. Being there every day reminded me of how fat and ugly I was. No one ever said that to me, of course, but my social anxiety was so crippling that I could never manage staff nights out and always found an excuse to avoid the Christmas party or anybody's leaving drinks. I knew that no matter how dolled up I would get, around these stunners I'd still look like a character from *Little Britain*.

I know that by separating myself from all social events it meant people didn't really get to know me and therefore I remained a grey area with a lot of the staff over the years. Both times when Frank was overseas, the people at work were supportive and gave me time off whenever I needed it and made sure everything was okay. And I never dropped my mask. I made out everything was SUPER.

After the wedding was over and I was losing more of a grasp on my moods and sanity, I found working at SPIN to be one of the toughest parts of my life. For the time I was there I needed to be at least 110 per cent at all times. I needed to be OMG AMAZE HILAR when I couldn't even manage a smile. I was so locked into the self-conscious battering of myself that I struggled even to just communicate. It made me seem cold and distant and yet all I craved was my co-workers' acceptance. I couldn't be the real me, though. My career had been built on a bubbly, upbeat voice. I couldn't let people know the truth that behind that put-on voice was a fragile, broken and frightened girl.

There was one voice that boomed louder than most in the building and provided some comfort to me – that was 98FM's sports guy, Johnny Lyons. (SPIN 1038 and 98FM shared the same building so we all integrated.) Johnny was always full of compliments. You couldn't pass Johnny without a smile. He was loud, warm-hearted and would give you the shirt off his back. Johnny wasn't like most people – if you tried to slip past him quietly he would follow you down the corridor with arms outstretched for a big hug. He had an unbelievable talent for making people feel good, not to mention an incredible broadcasting presence.

When I first spoke out about my depression and suicide attempts, Johnny sought me out and said he never knew I had gone through all of it. 'Fair play, Nikki, you are a soldier, marching the corridor of life and looking lovely in your lemon ensemble today.'

That was a typical remark from Johnny. He made me smile. (I'm even smiling here now as I type.) I was wearing a yellow top that day but he made it sound so much better than it was.

No matter what your form, you would always leave Johnny with a smile on your face.

I remember taking Farah in to meet everyone in work when she was a few weeks old. Johnny made such a fuss over her.

'What's this young lady's name?'

'Farah Rose – but we're just calling her Farah.'

He grinned. 'Farah Rose it is then. Farah Rose, in years to come your parents won't be letting you talk to the likes of me.'

When I had returned to work six months after her birth with post-natal depression, I made my bosses and the staff aware of my state of mind. He caught me on the stairs one day.

'Nikki with the smile so bright,' he said. 'Come here to me. Hug it out of you. How's the beautiful Farah Rose?'

'We only call her Farah, Johnny.'

'Farah Rose wouldn't want her mammy bawling now, would she?'

I wasn't bawling at that moment in time but I knew what he meant. For a man who towered above me and would drown out a crowd with his booming voice, he had a very soft centre.

Through Frank's deployment to Syria, when I was home alone with Farah, Johnny would always ask me how I was any time he saw me. He was like a paternal figure at work, taking me under his wing.

Then I got a text message one morning in August 2015 from Shona Ryan, the programme director of SPIN 1038. I read it:

> We are shocked to learn of Johnny Lyons' father's passing.

It didn't say that, but my mind had already translated it into the most likely text. Then I read it again, and again, and again, and again. It actually said:

> We are shocked to learn of Johnny Lyons' passing.

I couldn't believe it.

Shock. That was the feeling in the building. The building seemed to echo. No one could believe the news. He had been off with a leg injury but had only been in the week before. I don't know how he died and I don't want to know. I only want to remember the vibrant aura, the man who never stopped. At the time I thought everyone had got it wrong. That was the only reasonable explanation. Johnny Lyons could not be dead – plain and simple. Yet everyone said that he was. Tributes poured in over social media.

Eventually I had to accept it. He was gone.

I felt a huge sense of loss. My post-natal depression had reached an all-time low, so the news of Johnny's death hit me hard. A book of condolences was opened at the office. His photo was placed at reception and candles flickered beside it.

I was due to be on air the morning of his funeral, so the day before I drove into the city to the funeral home. It was a closed casket. I was the only one there at the time. I remember staring at the coffin. It seemed ginormous. His photo sat on top. My head tried to comprehend the fact that he was in there. I couldn't accept it.

I sat with him for over an hour, I chatted to him and I

did feel his presence. You can't have a light shine that bright without leaving some glow behind. My heart was heavy when I left the funeral home.

It had been arranged that the next day, at exactly midday, all commercial radio stations from SPIN 1038 to Today FM would play Johnny's favourite song, Prince's 'Purple Rain'. He was due to leave the church at that time.

At midday the next day I pulled up my mic and spoke. 'A few days ago, we lost a colleague, a great man who stood tall with the biggest heart. I lost a good friend. He has left a hole in our lives that cannot be filled. It's with huge sadness that I dedicate this song to Johnny Lyons. We miss you. Rest in peace.'

I hit play on the song and broke down crying.

Johnny's death affected me hugely. He was a larger-than-life character who had reached out to me when I was struggling. You didn't consider the possibility of Johnny dying; he had such a large presence and positive aura that life without him seemed incomprehensible. There wasn't a corner of the malt house building that didn't reverberate with his sound.

Afterwards, we all stood around his desk, said a few words, cried a lot and all together knocked back a shot of Jack Daniels, which had been his favourite drink. I absorbed the crippling grief of Jamie Moore, Stephen Doyle and Denis Vavasour, his closest friends, and I went to the back stairway of the building to cry my eyes out.

In the days after his death, I found my thoughts circling around the fact that he was gone, the shock of it, and I got more and more depressed.

What's the point if you can just be taken at any time with no warning?

My mood became toxic towards life and living. I was a fragile egg with the cracks beginning to show. It was only going to take one more thing to tip me over.

39

BREAKING UNDER THE RAINBOW

Nothing in life is free.
Well, love is.

Steven Courtney

The date came in late August 2015 for the Wales versus Ireland rugby match at the Aviva Stadium. Frank had arranged to go to see the match with one of the girls he'd been overseas with, along with some of her friends. I was relaxed about this situation because I knew she wasn't interested in men and so wouldn't take him away from me. I drove him in to the match, came home, played with Farah and put her to bed.

On my own, I began to feel very manic and started to pace the floor. My mood was extremely low because of something that had happened the day before. I'd heard that a friend of mine from 2FM was being replaced and I had texted him, saying:

Ehhhh, where are you off to?

I was being light-hearted and cheeky. He'd responded:

> Why, what did you hear?

> That one of our girls has gone to 2FM to take over your show. I wondered where you were moving to.

I'd heard nothing more from him and due to the innocence of the conversation I gave it no more thought, until I received a text later that day from him:

> You were right, Im off to weekends – press release going out at 4.

I felt unbelievably awful. I would never have asked the question if I thought he didn't know. I'd lost my job before with no warning. I would never forget the pain it caused and here was one of my closest confidantes in radio having something similar happen to him and I was the one to break the news. I'd presumed everyone knew, but it turns out the schedule change hadn't been mentioned to anyone and I'd found out purely by chance. I texted him back:

> Holy shit I had no idea you didn't know.

Knowing me for so long, he knew how I would be feeling and so he called me. He said he had heard it from others and all was good, so there was no need to be worried. I relaxed a little but still, deep down, I hated the fact that I had caused any pain to anyone, unintentionally or not.

Now, a day later, those feelings rose up once again.

Frank called me from the match. He was going to grab a few beers with the girls after it was over.

'That's fine. Farah's in bed.'

After he hung up I felt like I was about to burst out crying and didn't know why. All the events of the last few months were catching up with me. I began to shake and felt scared. What was wrong with me?

I sat down and decided to text an apology to Tina – the DJ who was taking over my friend's show – for breaking her news to my friend and perhaps causing trouble.

My phone pinged.

> What happened yesterday was not right … I realise you were shafted years ago … But Nikki there is a better way of giving someone a heads up.

My heart dropped. I felt so down in the dumps, I wanted to just disappear. I cared so deeply about what others thought of me and now they'd think I was a troublemaker who intentionally set out to sabotage a schedule change.

I tried to explain myself by text message. I apologised profusely and felt myself getting uncontrollably upset. Then my phone rang. It was Tina. I had worked with her over the years; she knew me and I'm sure she could see from the texts that I was very upset. She wanted to talk it through with me.

By the end of the conversation we had left it with huge congratulations from me to her and we hung up on friendly terms.

But not long afterwards the negative feelings about myself took over again. I started shaking uncontrollably. I couldn't stop crying. I was distraught. I felt like right there and then that all I wanted was silence. I just wanted to end my meaningless existence.

40

THE CRUSHED EFFECT

I just want it all to end.
I have had enough.

Anon

My phone rang again. It was Frank checking in on me.

'I'll be home soon. Are you okay?'

I don't know if it's instinct but every time I'm working extra hard to cover my feelings he always seems to know. My voice quivered.

'I'm not feeling great.'

'What? Why? What's wrong?'

'I'm a horrible person. I want to go. You'll be better off without me.' The crying turned to sobs. 'I can't do this any more. I don't want to do this any more. I'm so tired.'

Frank rushed home, but it was too late. I had taken a knife to my body and swallowed a pile of medication. I wanted to die, I wanted to not hear any more, not feel any more. I wanted peace from my own mind. I couldn't function; I couldn't even remember how to open the fridge. It was like my mind just gave up and switched off.

An ambulance was called. When it arrived I begged to see Farah one more time. They took me to her, sleeping in her cot. I said goodbye, as I didn't plan to come back. I remember the kind men from Dublin Fire Brigade, who run the ambulance service in my area, carrying me into the ambulance. I panicked then, aware that I was out of control and not sure what I was going to do. I had a feeling that something bad was going to happen – but of course it already had.

I was brought by ambulance to James Connolly Memorial Hospital (JCM). When I arrived I was assessed by the ER team and put on a drip immediately. I continued to try to harm myself and get away. I pulled the drip from my arm, blood spraying everywhere.

I need to get out of here now.

And go where?

Run. Run as fast as I can. To the bridge and jump off onto the M50. There'd be no way I'd survive that fall.

And then the silence I'd prayed for would come.

I was having this conversation in my head. It was like two people screaming at each other, neither making sense.

The doctor saw me getting agitated and tried to give me something to keep me relaxed until the psych team arrived to assess me. They managed to re-administer the drip and put a security guard standing by my bed to make sure I didn't pull it out again. Frank had called his parents, who were driving down from Donegal to be with us.

I went to the toilet and, while there, I made a break for it. I got through the first set of doors into the waiting area and bolted for the front entrance. Nurses and the security guard ran after me, and the security guard caught me before I reached the entrance. He said he would call the gardaí if I left the building, as I was a danger to myself.

Frank and the security guard managed to coax me back in and the psychiatrist-on-call said they were holding me under the Mental Health Act. I now legally could not leave the hospital without permission from a doctor.

41

UNDER LOCK AND KEY

... it is sometimes satisfying to cut yourself and bleed. On those gray days where eight in the morning looks no different than noon and nothing has happened and nothing is going to happen and you are washing a glass in the sink and it breaks – accidentally – and punctures your skin. And then there is the red shock, the brightest thing in the day, so vibrant it buzzes, this blood of yours. That is okay sometimes because at least you know you're alive.

Augusten Burroughs, *Running with Scissors*

I was so tired. I wanted to go home.

Everything's okay now.

I had always believed that if I said these words everyone would believe me and everything would go back to normal. I was delusional, of course, but I still said this to Frank. 'Everything's okay.'

He couldn't believe what he was hearing. How on earth could I think that everything could just switch back after what had happened? Cutting myself, trying to kill myself, crying because I couldn't open the fridge.

Mental health is so fragile. I have lived with the extremes

of mental health, the highs and the lows, most of my life. The ups, the downs, the swinging moods. The all or nothing effect. The 'I love you' or 'I hate you' attitude. Frank had, of course, witnessed this over the years. The first major sign, for him, that things weren't as they seemed on the surface with me, was when he found me one day standing, distraught and inconsolable, over a saucepan of water. I had been crying into the saucepan because the water wouldn't boil. At the time it had seemed like the most devastating thing in the world to me.

Over the next few days in hospital I was put under the care of Dr Kirrane. It was during this period – being held under the Mental Care Act – that I was finally diagnosed with BPD. I had never heard of it before. It was never a diagnosis that had been discussed. Doctors throughout the years had interpreted my illness as things like 'depression', 'eating disorder', 'body dysmorphia' and 'anxiety'.

Dr Kirrane sat me down with her team and explained the course of action. I was going to be staying as an inpatient until they figured out my recovery plan. I would get privileges, as I earned them, like being able to go to the shop upstairs.

I cried for two solid days. I will never ever forget the kindness and patience shown to me by the nursing staff in the Ash Psychiatric Ward in JCM during this time. They made me feel like I might be able to make sense of all that was whirling about in my head. They showed me affection, held me when I cried and wiped my tears. They helped me get used to my new medications, which made me very sleepy. I attended occupational therapy and psychology as an inpatient and because I was continually reopening my wounds with my nails (I wanted to keep feeling the pain), I spent a lot of time in First Aid being bandaged back up.

As in most psychiatric wards, I had my laces, my hair straightener, phone charger, belts – anything that could be considered a weapon I might use on myself – confiscated. My make-up bag was taken because of the mirror, which could be used as a sharp object if broken.

After a few days the crying subsided and I grew calmer from the medication. I walked up the ward, examining my new surroundings. There were people from all different walks of life. People battling addictions, personality disorders, severe depression, schizophrenia, psychosis. Poor mental health most definitely doesn't have a type, nor is it choosy. We were all suffering through our own individual crises.

After a week it was agreed by the doctors that I could go on supervised trips upstairs to the coffee shop. It meant I could leave the ward under Frank's supervision for a small amount of time. I felt disorientated the first day. I thought everyone was looking at us pityingly, as if they knew what had happened. I believed they were looking at me, thinking I was:

A psycho.

A bad wife.

A bad mother.

All this criticism blasted loud and harsh from my own voice inside my head.

I didn't want to be here. I wanted to go home. I cried and pleaded with Frank but he said I wasn't coming home until the doctors had figured out my recovery plan and it was safe to leave me alone again. Farah had been taken up to her grandparents' house while I was in hospital, as Frank was finding it hard enough to juggle hospital visits with work. Farah adored her grandparents and so, no matter how guilty I felt, at least I knew she was safe and happy. She cried a few times for me, Mary told me later on that year, and it pulled on my heart thinking about how I had left my baby behind.

42

FEEL THE FEAR AND DO IT ANYWAY

Mental illness is not a choice
But hope is.

Nikki Hayes

Frank called my bosses and told them everything. They were clearly shocked, as I hadn't displayed any signs of distress at work. As usual, I had kept on my happy face, even as I drowned under the surface. They assured him that they would not disclose any details about why I was absent and wished me a speedy recovery. I disappeared from social media, I faded into the background, and only those very close to me knew what was going on. I was lucky to have a great husband and a great friend in Audrey as she accompanied Frank to the hospital a few times.

I remember the main thing that the people close to me seemed to feel was shock. They also felt bad that they didn't spot anything. I didn't even know that things were so bad, really – not while I was going through it. Looking back, yes, the signs were there, but I couldn't see them at the time, blinded as I was by self-hatred and my own self-destruct mission.

I had been in work the Friday before the breakdown. My bosses said I was in exceptionally good form. Always pushing hardest when I'm running low on steam. Friends said they'd talked to me and I was in high spirits, so no one had seen the crash coming, but it had been inevitable once I started falling.

BANG.

I was gone.

Taking my medication every day in the Ash Ward ensured my mood was good, stable and that the impulsive, reckless thoughts were kept away. These medications are sedative, so they give me the time to work things out before I act. When I first took them after my breakdown I was very slurred and delayed, but I have since caught up. My memory can be a little forgetful but then Frank says I always was a little scatter-brained. The mood stabiliser that I also take ensures that I don't swing from highs to lows. The only side effect that I have really noticed, bar the forgetfulness, is that I haven't cried in a long time. I'm not sure if that's a good or bad thing – though in the past I did cry too much. I admit, for now, that I need to be medicated, but I am hopeful that I will reach some point in the future where I will be able to manage my illness without the aid of medication.

I have found humour gets me through a lot of difficult times, especially over the last two years since my breakdown. Being locked away in the basement of a hospital for seven weeks can affect you. I found dark humour helped me through some moments. I had a lot of time to think. I had more time than I knew what to do with. It didn't matter what I looked like because no one could see me and I had no mirror to try to fix my face anyway. I remember getting quite defeated at this fact, only to look up and see a massive spider cowering in the corner of the shower in my room. As I washed the wounds on my arms, which were still bleeding from my picking at them, I looked at the spider and felt a connection. *Of all the showers you could turn up in, mate, you turn up on the psych ward.*

I laughed a little inside at the tragedy of it all, at first, and then I felt sorry for the spider who, I convinced myself, was also depressed. The spider stayed there for about a week and then disappeared. I wasn't sure if he'd been discharged or simply made a break for it.

I also discovered art therapy when I was in for my long stay on the Ash Ward, as they provided inpatient occupational therapy, which is the use of certain activities to help with recuperation from mental illness. This was my saving grace. I looked forward to art classes and cookery classes, as well as my favourite day when the therapy dog was brought down to the ward – a beautiful golden retriever whose snuggles and licks, I'm convinced, had healing properties.

I was only a week in when Frank brought me in some colouring pencils and an adult colouring book. I thought he was the mad one. When he went, though, I started on a few pages and realised, when I'd finished, that the call for medication was on. I'd become absorbed in the task. It had certainly helped pass the time.

As the weeks progressed, I found art therapy to be my saviour. I started on a canvas in the art class, a large one that I'd be able to hang at home whenever I was discharged. I spray-painted the canvas gold and started making little butterfly shapes out of patterned paper. I looked through books and magazines for quotes and cut them out to add to my project. It became a positive focus for me; every day I added to it a little more. I got great satisfaction from every bit of progress that I made and was very proud of my efforts. As it turned out, once I was done with mine, I started helping other patients with theirs, which was also gratifying.

I have carried this newly discovered arts and crafts element of my personality home with me since being discharged. I love nothing more than creating gifts and making keepsakes. I recently finished 3D frames with our family tree for Frank's family. I'm so happy with the end result and know for a fact that they are unique.

Having outlets is a big thing with mental illness. Diverting your mind for long enough from triggers that start a negative pattern can get you through difficult times. This is why occupational therapy is an important element of recovery for those suffering from BPD.

After three weeks as an inpatient on the Ash Ward, my doctors wanted me to attempt a few hours at home to see how I got on. I was nervous about leaving the ward, worried that when people saw me they'd think I was a lunatic. I was also scared that I might not be able to control another self-hatred attack if I should feel manic.

Once we arrived at the house Frank opened the front door and led me into the sitting-room. He held me tightly on the couch. We spoke about what had happened and how we were both feeling. After a few hours I found myself increasingly panicked and asked Frank to take me back to the ward. It was only while walking down the stairs and back into the familiar clinical surroundings of the ward that I relaxed again. I was safe now. I couldn't harm myself.

The doctors were disappointed that I didn't have a successful day, but they quickly geared me up for another visit the following week. They suggested that Frank's parents bring Farah back down to see me. I missed her so much, so I agreed. I didn't know what to expect. Would she be frightened of me? Had she forgotten me?

I woke the following Saturday, excited. Frank was coming to pick me up around lunchtime and we were going to meet his parents and Farah at the Dunboyne Castle Hotel not far from the hospital. We chose the venue as we didn't want her seeing me in the hospital and felt if we went back to the house it might confuse her and she'd want to stay. She had to get back on the road with her nana and granda, so we wanted to make sure it was as stress-free as possible for her. I couldn't wait to see my little girl and, at the same time, I was dreading seeing my in-laws because I wasn't sure if they'd understand where I was coming from or even want to know.

I couldn't have been more wrong. They were cheerful, distracting me from what was going on by chatting about all that Farah had gotten up to while she'd been staying with them.

She'd met all her cousins and taken part in a family sports day, where she won a medal. I was missing out on so much. We had a light lunch and after that it was time for me to head back to the ward. I said goodbye with my heart in tatters. I wanted to take my baby home and cuddle her; instead I was saying goodbye again and heading back under lockdown.

The day had gone well, the nurses were happy with my report, and so I got into bed and allowed the powerful exhaustion I felt to take me to sleep.

The next week, my fifth week on the ward, I decided to tell people where I was and why. Maybe it would help me to be honest and, in turn, it would help others too. I spoke to Frank and we both agreed that something simple but to the point would do.

I placed the camera of my phone on my leg and snapped. The picture was of my feet at the end of the bed and of the surrounding ward. It was clear that I was in hospital. I added the text:

> A month ago I had an acute mental breakdown. I am in hospital recovering #itsoknottobeok

I put my phone away and slept for quite some hours that day. I was drained. At the same time, I knew I was making progress. I was finally being honest and was getting a chance to be me.

43

FALLING BEYOND THE WILL TO LIVE

People who need help sometimes look a lot like people who don't need help.

Glennon Doyle Melton

I can honestly say when I broke down that I was scattered all over the place. I didn't think I would ever be put back together. It's like I was a smashed mirror and even if you somehow managed to glue me back together I'd still be broken.

I had spent the majority of my life feeling worthless and sad. I spent most of my life hating who I was and wishing I was someone else. I spent the majority of my life shouting abuse at myself. When I had the chance to create someone new through work, I found the pressure of balancing the two personalities (along with the countless other masks that I wore) too much and inevitably cracked and broke.

I would love a break from my own racing thoughts – I would love silence in my mind – an escape from the constant nagging and criticising voice: *you're fat, you're ugly, your nose is big, your stomach is flabby, your hair looks shit.* Yet, contradictorily, silence is also the very thing that I fear. If my mind were silent, I would most likely feel uncomfortable. As a result, I would act ill-at-ease around people and the focus would be on me. If the focus turned to me, I believed everyone would see me for the fraud I am. This is how my mind works.

It's never-ending, from the moment I wake up until I go to sleep. Sometimes, even in my dreams, I am a waste of space.

The medications that I am currently on do slow my thoughts down slightly but they're no miracle cure. The chastising continues. I can be so cruel and damaging to myself. No one can ever hurt me in the way that I can hurt myself. I think, on some level, I feel that if I'm the one causing the harm to myself then I am somehow protected from the hurt other people can cause me. It's harder to hurt someone who's already in pain.

I've spent so much time trying to understand my disorder but it's so complex and ever changing, so keeping up with it can prove difficult.

My life so far has played out in episodes:

1) Childhood
2) Teenage years
3) First suicide attempt
4) College
5) Second suicide attempt
6) New York

7) Sane time or at least unmedicated

8) Crazy time/successful career-wise

9) The deaths, particularly that of my father

10) Me going off the rails

11) Finding out who my friends were

12) My breakdown

Now I am in the aftermath of that. My recovery has been slow and in stages. I have slipped back and, unbeknownst to most people – bar my bosses and my team of doctors – I have had two further stays on the Ash Ward this year, once for a week and then for two days.

Recovery doesn't mean everything is rosy all the time; but it does mean that when I fall I can get back up quicker and the aftermath isn't quite so destructive.

44

MENTAL HEALTH ISN'T PICKY

People who are not good for you may be closer than you think. Protect yourself by building and maintaining healthy boundaries.

Anon

Through my treatment I have met some really amazing people and heard stories that are all so different, yet so alike.

Spending almost seven weeks in close sleeping quarters you get to know each other's behaviours and mannerisms. Some people weren't ready to start living and still tried to end their pain, some people screamed their frustrations until they were medicated to sleep, some people were angry and paced the corridor for hours, some people believed they would be going home soon and tried to keep their hopes alive.

I will cherish the individual relationships that I made when I was an inpatient, both last year and earlier this year. The nurses were familiar, reassuring faces with arms open wide, and even the cleaning staff were supportive. Some of the girls from my ward stay in touch with a message of support here and there. All of us continue fighting to live and be happy.

I know some people have an image of psychiatric wards as a place where people shuffle dazed along the walls or drool from being overly medicated, but this really isn't so. Patients come from all walks of life. There were vets, accountants, mums, dads, sons, daughters – all different and yet all with a common sadness.

Don't judge someone if they need psychiatric care. You don't know if one episode in your life might lead you to needing the service. I never judge anyone. I don't believe that I have the right to. People don't just end up at the end of a story – something has led them to the point where you notice them. People don't just become addicts, don't just become criminals, don't just become homeless – their journey has broken down along the road. Be mindful.

I understand from being at the top of the ladder, and the bottom, that the only person you cannot escape is yourself, so you have to try to love yourself. I am sure I'll never love myself entirely – that would be a miracle – but I am trying to like myself, and I hope that after a few years of therapy and treatment I will be able to get to that place.

There are times when I don't want to share my experiences but I always stop myself and remind myself that I have a responsibility. I am in the public eye and if I don't use my career to highlight something so crucial to this country, then I am failing in my position. I have had moments where all I want to do is go to Twitter and type:

Will someone help me? I can't go on.

But instead I work through those moments with my family and medical team and then, after figuring it out properly, I write about how I felt and how I came out the other end.

Remain hopeful. This is the message I wish to portray. Yes, you can feel down in the dumps; yes, you can hate yourself to the point of self-harm, but remember #itsoknottobeok. If I can get through it, then so can you.

I have been blogging for a while now and the feedback I get from others suffering in silence is what propels me on. I can't sit back and enjoy the perks of media and ignore the fact that I have a front-stage podium that I can use to try to get a better mental health service in this country and to get people talking. And the only way to raise awareness is to get people talking.

The greatest privilege I have had since speaking out about my mental state of mind is hearing other people's stories. I remember meeting a girl who, on the surface and in my eyes, had it all. She was beautiful, had a great body and worked in a good job. Then she confided in me that she suffered with bulimia and had self-harmed because she was sick of being big-chested. She wanted a reduction operation but couldn't afford it and was filled with hatred every time a man made a lewd comment towards her. You'd look at this girl and think she had the world, but all she wanted to do was fade into the background.

Another time I spoke to a woman who had a great career

but still tried to take her own life twenty-six times. The first few times she wanted the pain to stop. She couldn't bear to live with the excruciating pain of existence every day. She spent time in and out of hospital, always visiting different hospitals so a case file was never fully built on her. She slipped through the loopholes of the health system in Ireland. She was being held under the Mental Health Act when she escaped and jumped off a bridge. She survived with a broken leg. She constantly self-harmed and lived in a pool of guilt for the hurt and shame that she felt she brought to her family. It took a while for her to open up to me, but once she did she didn't stop.

What caused her to feel this way?

I asked that in my head as I heard her story, so I know you must have too. She was ill. She couldn't handle her swinging moods, her episodes of mania, or her split personality. She was drowning in herself and was desperately screeching for help. Yet when we spoke over a game of Jenga for an hour in the ward all I saw was a frightened little girl who wanted her mammy and daddy and wanted someone to take care of her for a while. She was someone who, through no fault of her own, had fallen into a few destructive relationships. She was drifting through life unregulated and all she needed was care and time. I grew very fond of her during the time we spent together. As she didn't want to keep in contact after she left I just pray that she's alive and well today.

I have met people who have been beaten by their partner, emotionally abused by their loved ones, or sexually abused by those they trusted. I've also met people, like me, who developed emotional instability. There are so many reasons why someone can develop BPD. Don't always assume that your loved one is being dramatic, attention-seeking or difficult. Everyone has their bad days but take it from me – sufferers of personality disorders don't get bad days. We get bad weeks, months and years.

45

DEEP DOWN INSIDE

The body is wise, the confusion is from the mind.

Aniekee Tochukwu Ezekiel

It is impossible to fully imagine what goes through someone's mind when they contemplate suicide. I have had a few suicide attempts and there's never usually a sign. For me, the impulsivity associated with BPD is what takes over. I become overwhelmed, I panic, and the natural progression of this is that I feel I need to die. Each time I have made an attempt on my life everything has seemed reasonably okay up to the moment I fall over the cliff. I have lost a few friends to suicide and with each one of them all seemed calm until they were gone.

I know, for me, that when I am consumed with pain, confusion and self-loathing I forget everything bar the uncontrollable urge to hurt myself or remove myself from a world that I feel I am unworthy of inhabiting. I've heard people say that suicide is selfish and the coward's way out. It may seem that way, but when you feel the world is so dark that you're drowning, then you don't think rationally. You don't see the support or love that may surround you. You just feel unbearable pain and a longing for peace.

Taking your own life is – in my experience – rarely something you decide to do with meticulous planning. It's often the only way you can see the pain stopping. People who commit suicide don't necessarily want their lives to end; they simply want to end their pain. I always feel if there was a way of making people realise this – rather than clinging to the current stigma that still lies around mental health – then we may be able to intervene more often when someone becomes so desperate that ending their life is seen as their only option. Each time I have attempted to kill myself, I felt certain it was my only option. I needed to stop the noise in my head, the constant battles between my various different personalities.

A lot of times suicide becomes more of an option when your inhibitions are lowered. One of my friends hung himself while under the influence of alcohol. Twice this had proven true for me. Drink is a depressant and for someone who is already acutely depressed this can lead to your condition becoming unmanageable. It is when you are uninhibited that you often begin to contemplate suicide.

I'd like to say that you stop and think about those you are leaving behind and how it will impact on them. You do in a way, I suppose, but you don't think of them being sad or tortured. You convince yourself that everyone – and that includes your nearest and dearest – will be happier and better off once you have left this world.

I've never written a letter, I've never shown signs. When

I've made attempts on my life they have been spontaneous and driven by crippling pain inside.

People ask me a lot – 'How could I have known? How could someone have stopped you?' I have addressed these questions a lot with my psychologist. There is a pattern, but unfortunately it's a pattern that the person suffering with the disorder can't identify clearly enough to be able to stop it. Friends or family who know someone well might learn to identify the symptoms, but even when they do it is almost impossible for them to convince the sufferer that they are on a downward spiral and need help.

I can only speak for myself, but the first time I attempted to take my own life I was a teenager. Hormones were racing and I had an awful body image struggle. I hated myself and struggled with who I was. I desperately wanted to be thin and pretty, and because I couldn't change my looks I decided to focus on my body and so developed an eating disorder.

I understand a lot of those feelings are what most teens go through, but the difference with me was that I was already mentally unstable. Had I been diagnosed with a mood disorder at this time would it have changed anything? I don't know, to be honest; I was hell-bent on making myself into a new me. A more improved, better me. Someone that people would like. I guess my impulsivity could have been controlled with medication, but then again the only warning signs before my first suicide attempt were the ones flying around my mind. Everything on the outside seemed calm. I was painfully shy and self-conscious. I never had boyfriends and if someone were ever to show interest in me I would cut them out of my life, as it was a feeling that made me very uncomfortable. I believed what my mind told me. *I'm obese, I'm ugly, I'm nothing.* That mantra repeating day and night in a teenager's mind is most definitely a weapon.

We didn't talk about mental health in the 1990s in Ireland, so I quickly got myself the nickname 'Frigid Bridget' on our estate. This added to my self-hatred. Why couldn't I be like the others and just go with boys? Why did I have to have such frizzy hair and so many freckles?

I didn't feel happy that time, waking up in hospital after my overdose. I felt trapped and ashamed that I didn't manage to complete what I had set out to do. There was also guilt for making my parents have to deal with it. I was lower than I'd ever felt before.

When I look back at the multiple times that I have made an attempt to end my life, I can see that I was manic, frantic, overwhelmed and absolutely convinced that everyone would be better off if I were removed from this world. It was relentless; I just wanted to get out.

When I went to college I created a persona that couldn't be sustained long-term. I was a wound-up toy that never stopped, 24/7, giving life 110 per cent. There was an inevitable crash and burn, especially when I had no support network nearby.

The abuse of substances like alcohol and narcotics added to the frenzy. I tried everything. Then I fell. I ran out of money, I ran out of steam, I ran out of stories and costumes. I ran out of life. The suicide attempt in college was most definitely assisted by substance abuse, but I refused help. Even when I was being told I was very ill I ran from the care of the hospital and pushed my body and mind to the point where I collapsed and had a seizure.

Again, that time, I didn't want to be saved; I wanted to disappear. I wanted to be laid out inside my coffin, asleep. The thought of that image, the thought of that silent feeling, had filled me with joy. I'm not telling you this to make you feel sorry for me, I'm just trying to help you understand why someone who is suffering can take the drastic step of ending their life.

46

RECOVERY

Sharing my hell and showing my scars is the most frightening and rewarding experience ever.

Nikki Hayes

With me there is no happy ever after. There is no miraculous cure meaning that suddenly I will never have a bad day again. I live with this now. Just like someone who has diabetes, I have Borderline Personality Disorder/Emotionally Unstable Personality Disorder.

I take medication every single day – five pills in the morning, two at teatime and four more in the evening. I also attend weekly appointments with my psychologist. It's a great deal of work, trying to figure out a lifetime of confusion. I see my consultant psychiatrist once every six weeks and I have a mental health nurse assigned to me when I need one.

BPD isn't something that just goes away once it is diagnosed, but it does become a lot easier to deal with it once you have the right help. Having a support system in place changes things.

47

FEEDBACK

Trying to explain mental illness to someone who's never experienced it is like trying to explain colour to a blind person.

Unknown

The amazing thing about being able to speak out now about my illness is that we, as a society, appear ready to listen. I first spoke out around 2003 about my depression and initial suicide attempt. I had read in the newspaper about a fellow DJ, Gareth O'Callaghan, opening up about his battle with depression and, after talking to him about my own battles, he encouraged me to speak out in public. But people weren't ready to listen then; it was still a taboo.

I'll always remember a friend's funeral where there was no mention of him taking his life, no mention of his male partner – it was like the priest and family were just ignoring who he was and portraying him as someone completely different. I felt very uncomfortable about this and sad for his partner, who was grieving alone.

When I have spoken out in the past, certain people listened, but it never made much of an impact. That has changed over the last two years. As a society we are ready to admit our weaknesses and shortfalls. We are ready to hold up our hands and say, 'I'm not actually doing too good' #itsoknottobeok.

I remember tweeting that hashtag five years ago and it meant nothing. Now Twitter predicts the hashtag as you type it.

Gareth O'Callaghan was the first person I ever heard speak publicly about mental illness. His words struck a chord with me. I spoke with him in 2004 and he said the world was ready to talk about other people's mental illness but not about their own and certainly not about their brother who tripped climbing a tree and got caught up in his scarf. We were deluded as a nation and thought that ignorance was bliss.

But this wasn't something that was going away. With the crash in our economy many high-flyers came crashing to earth and 'depression' became the buzzword.

Step forward Niall Breslin, i.e. Bressie. When Bressie talked out about his journey with mental health issues people stopped and listened. I don't know if it was the combination of him being a good-looking, successful music star with a TV career that did it, but I thank God for the day that Niall Breslin sat down and decided to share his story with us. Ever since that breakthrough he has gone on to raise huge amounts of money and awareness for mental health in Ireland.

I spoke with Bressie at the Under the Mask Ball in Croke Park in 2015 that had been organised by Sam Osbourne to highlight mental health and in memory of Keith Cooper, who played for St Sylvester's and the Parnells GAA team. It was like a Debs, with all the young adults decked out in the best of gear. The theme was 'under the mask', which was meant to symbolise the stigma surrounding mental health in Ireland. Bressie and I were asked to speak before the music, while the students were mid-dinner. Bressie spoke of success and pain. How things can seem great on the outside and yet you can be torn apart on the inside. The teenage audience connected immediately. The fact that we told them that at least one person sitting at their table would be affected with mental health issues at some stage in their lives shocked them.

I remember feeling a burst of pride after that event. People were starting to listen. I really felt mental health in Ireland was turning a massive corner and it was only by people in the public eye continuously sharing their stories and struggles that some sort of normality could be achieved.

Two particular stories stick in my mind that highlight how sharing your stories can make a difference. The first one sent me into tears as soon as I received the email. It relates to an appearance I made on TV3's *Ireland AM* show. Sinead Desmond, Mark Cagney and the whole Ireland AM crew have been so supportive of me. I had participated in a mental health special series earlier in the year for TV3, and when they asked me back for National Suicide Awareness Week I was only too happy to appear. I spoke about my own journey with self-harm and how it led from small cuts to hospital admissions to overdoses that should have killed me. I spoke to a younger me and pleaded with her to share, talk, stop covering up. The interview was less than four minutes but it made a difference.

I went in to do my radio show that day after the TV appearance. I was feeling a little vulnerable, which was normal after I publicly shared. I put on my smile and three hours later handed over to the next shift. I was starting to feel the effects of the early start and was quite tired. I checked my emails, as always, before leaving for home and that's when I saw the email with the subject 'Thank you'.

I glanced at the name. It didn't mean anything. *It must be a PR company*, I thought. I decided to open it and have a glance before I left the office.

An hour later I was still rooted to my chair, tears in my eyes and suffering from that horrible stiff jaw you get when you are trying to hold back tears. A young woman had been affected by the downturn in the economy. She was earning less money, could be losing her house to the bank and her relationship with her husband was strained. This woman was in a bad way. In the email she explained how that morning she had written a suicide note to her mother. Her mother picked her daughter up from school, so it was her mother who'd find her body. She explained the pain she was in and the fact that she felt that, by dying, she would be releasing the world of a burden. She told me she had enough pills to knock out a stable of horses and had them lined up in front of her on the table. The TV was on from before she dropped her daughter off to school. She had opened a bottle of alcohol. It had all been planned out, she told me in her email. She had decided how and where she would end her life. She had a clear plan and set of instructions that she was going to follow – she would do it this morning as she had four hours until her mother came back and therefore enough time for the medication to work through her and end her life.

She said I came on the TV as she sat there ready to die. She saw the banner on the bottom of the screen, which said I had tried to take my life. She tuned in. After I had told my story and spoken to the younger me, she broke down crying. She said she felt like I was speaking to her. She put the lid on the pills and poured the alcohol down the sink. She broke down crying into her hands and called her mum. Had I not been on *Ireland AM* that morning she would be dead. I had crossed the emotional barrier and translated a message of hope.

I felt so honoured to have been the one to talk her down. It does feel nice to know that you have made a change, that by sharing your deepest, darkest moments you have managed to show someone the path through to the other side.

There is one other story that I remember. This was around the time I was interviewed for the *Daily Mail* about my suicide attempts. I explained to them the thought process behind someone who has reached that point in their lives. I spoke from my experiences and my thoughts. After sharing, I didn't think about it again.

A few weeks later, I was scheduled to take a Toyota for a test drive. In order to pick up the car I had to get a taxi to Toyota HQ on the Killeen Road. I called a local taxi company. A woman answered with a very warm and friendly voice. I booked the cab and then she asked for my name.

'Nikki Hayes.'

'Nikki Hayes who was in the paper the other week? Are you on the radio?'

'Yes.'

'Thank you,' she said. I didn't know what I was being thanked for until she followed up with, 'We buried my brother a few weeks ago. It came out of nowhere; we all blamed ourselves. He hung himself and my parents took it particularly bad. We are just all in shock …'

'I'm so sorry for your loss.'

'Thank you, though. My mother read your article in the *Mail* and she seems to have connected with where his head was and knows it wasn't her fault. Thank you for speaking out.' Then she added, 'Now, that's your taxi booked.'

Sometimes, when you share, you forget that people listen. You are also never really sure that you'll make any kind of difference. So receiving such encouraging feedback shows me why I had to talk out, and why I must continue to do so.

48

CONFUSION OF BEING ME

Be careful what you say.
You can say something hurtful in ten seconds, but ten years later, the wounds are still there.

Joel Osteen

Maybe the most confusing part of BPD are the times that you go against yourself, running in the opposite direction to where you want to go.

I want you to love me so I'll push you away.

I want to be pretty so I'll cut through my flesh.

I want to be thin so I'll binge and make myself ill.

I want to go out so I'll hide under the duvet instead.

When people see this pattern in you, they can often think you are just being lazy and uncooperative (unless they know you are diagnosed).

'If you hate things that much just change it.'

'Get off your ass and go for a walk.'

I more than understand the benefits of taking control of

your thoughts but I also know that's not always the easiest thing to do with BPD. They race so fast that I often have difficulty making sense of them. I also know that exercise is encouraged and beneficial for your mental health but, for many, getting to the point where you can actually get up and get dressed is the main battle. If you can push yourself so hard that you can run a marathon, that's amazing, but for a lot of people with negative opinions of themselves, just putting on their trainers could cause a severe anxiety attack.

This need to exercise is something I've struggled with all my life – and as a result I've struggled with my weight. I always swing a stone or two up and down at different times of the year. When I'm weak and struggling to keep my head above water the thought of exercise fills me with dread – even the simplest task, like walking the dogs. I feel people will be looking at me, judging how I look, sneering at me. If someone laughs across the street I will think they're laughing at me.

Recently, as things have been going better for me mentally, Frank suggested I take some classes. My core is weak due to numerous surgeries on my abdominal area, as well as my C-section. I reluctantly signed up to my local gym and went in with Frank to get my ID card sorted. As we got out of the car in the car park, my heart was racing, my fists tight and clammy.

'Frank, this is my worst nightmare.'

'You'll be okay, hold my hand.'

We walked through the doors and I bowed my head in shame, seeing these toned and built up goddesses and gods. I looked down at my expanding waistline and thought I would die right then with shame. My heart was racing and I wanted to make a bolt for the door. I wanted to get away from the perceived disgust on people's faces as they looked at my podgy face.

'I'm so proud of you,' Frank said.

'I don't think you understand,' I whispered. 'This is my worst nightmare. I feel sick.'

He told me to look around and see the people who were trying hard to lose weight and get fit, but all I saw were bodybuilders and glamour girls. Even the sweaty brunette on the ski machine looked better than me. My morphed view of my appearance had me look in a mirror and see Shrek the ogre looking back – and not your typical Shrek, but Shrek after Christmas when he's fatter than normal.

One month in and I cancelled my membership and resigned myself to being fat and miserable. I have desperately wanted liposuction for years but can't afford it. I said it to Frank many times – I'd happily take out a loan and pay it back for the rest of my life if I could finally have the shape that I have always desired. This remains a dream and maybe someday I'll be able to do it. Going under the knife to look good would be a walk in the park for me.

49

SURVIVING RAW

Not until we are lost do we begin to understand ourselves.

Henry David Thoreau

People with BPD are emotionally raw. Every little moment stings. You feel it's important how people view you, how you act. You are constantly putting yourself under scrutiny to perform to the highest standard and you genuinely believe that the rest of the world sets these high standards – which of course you can never meet.

These inflexible and volatile beliefs caused immense stress to both my loved ones and me. I've been told in treatment that this damaging way of dealing with life is something that establishes itself in your younger years. I know that I developed an unhealthy balance of emotions from a young age: all or nothing; love or rejection; life or death.

I sometimes worry about Farah. Will she develop as I did? Will she be hurt by the world and hate herself? I wouldn't wish my emotional state on anyone and I will spend my life trying to protect her from it. I tell her I love her every moment of the day. Hugs are endless and she gets constant affection and assurance, both from myself and from Frank.

She is definitely being raised in a loving environment. I never raise my voice near Farah, even if I'm on the phone. I need her to know that this is an accepting home where she can be whoever she wants to be. I want her to see her mother as a strong person. I won't hide my illness from her when she's older. I'll sit her down and explain it. I'll keep fighting in the meantime so she will see that if her mammy can fight through all her troubles, then she will also be able to do so.

50

UNDERSTANDING WHO I'VE BECOME

I get up and pace the room, as if I can leave my guilt behind me. But it tracks me as I walk, an ugly shadow made by myself.

Rosamund Lupton, *Sister*

There are many challenges living with BPD. A massive one for me has always been that I suffer from anxiety when in groups. I can talk to tens of thousands of people from a stage in the Phoenix Park with no problems – I did this in 2003 – but stick me in a room with a handful of people and I panic. I wrote an email to my colleagues when I decided to go part-time after two years coming to terms with my BPD. Here's that email:

> For someone who never expresses my emotion in work often – be warned it's all going to come out here :)
>
> I'm not someone who communicates my emotion too well – it's all part of the mental illness. EUPD means when I want to show affection and warmth I close up and seem distant. When I talk over you, I don't mean to, it's a nervous

impulsive thing and I certainly don't mean to interrupt or seem rude. I say exactly what's in my head before thinking it through (Crossy you'll remember the lemons) – Frank calls it Homer Simpson Syndrome :)

That's the science behind me :) But now to where you all fit in in my life.

Spin has been a part of my life for 14 years. From the day Liam Thompson called me to tell me I got "the Gig" when I told him "I felt like I won the lotto" to when Liam and Jamie [Crawford] met me in 2010 to take me back to Spin Towers and back into what had remained a family to me even when I was at RTE.

I would always sit at the Spin table at the PPI's, Advertising Awards (where to Jamie's amusement/horror John Power gave me a piggy back around the hall of the Burlington in front of the nations media). Spins portacabin was always the one to be in at Festivals – constant beer supply and craic – it was always a place that people, including me, were drawn to.

I have been very sick over the last year and a half and Spin as a company and all of you guys have been the most amazing people possible. Calling and texting me when I'm out, to offers of hospital visits (Becki I never forget your kind words that time especially). One constant was Jamie's support no matter what happened – he always said "you first and then work" and he stood by that right through never making me feel pressured in my recovery. I've known Jamie since his late teens and saw him come in as a spini and progress to CEO – something he was always going to focus towards and get. I'll always be thankful for his support to Frank and I.

Now – this is what I want you all to know – you are a unique crew of people. All diverse with one common ground – Love. Spin isn't a workplace, it's your heart and soul which gives back as much as you give.

I am taking some time to focus on my family but I will still be around and friendships made will never be broken. It also means I'm now becoming ur audience ... cant wait to become a Spin listener :) and Georgie that means you will constantly be educating me on the lives and loves of the Kardashians which you fought the last few years to get through to me :) your patience was commendable and appreciated :)

And for all up the corridor – the love did extend past the vending machine – you guys are close to my heart and [I] will never forget the friendship and support you gave to me over the last year. Michael Brett – professionally and personally – you are a legend!!!

Spin will always be a part of me – enjoy every moment working for a unique, loving brand that is Spin 1038.

All my love always,
Nikki xxx

The crew on the floor at work were amazing. Many responded to my email, admitting that they had not realised the depth of the feelings that I was experiencing.

I know that the support I was shown was unique. Many

people have confided in me that their employers are less than supportive when they open up about their depression or anxiety problems. For example, a girl who shared my room with me in hospital had crippling depression. Her doctor had admitted her to hospital. She decided to be upfront and tell her employers exactly why she was being hospitalised. They didn't react too well and, rather than support her, they put her under immense pressure to return to work.

This is an area where the stigma surrounding mental health still exists in Ireland. If you were out sick with a bacterial chest infection you would turn in your sick note, rest and return to work when you are at your full strength again. But this is not the case with mental health issues. We definitely are getting better at it but a letter like this:

> Joe Soap is certified by me to be unfit for work due to panic attacks.
> Sincerely,
> Doctor Nick

well, it doesn't hold the same punch. It should, but it doesn't. Firstly, Doctor Nick would probably put down a viral illness instead as, sure, that covers a multitude of things and, secondly, Joe Soap won't want to seem weak to his employers. He'll want time to rest but he'll convince himself that the viral week will be enough.

But a week is not enough time to deal with a mental health illness. Recovery – both mentally and physically – takes time and care. Everyone is different. I don't think in my lifetime the stigma will fully lift regarding mental health but I do think that we have made huge progress and we are getting there.

51

PUTTING THE PIECES TOGETHER

We are neither on good terms or bad.
We are no longer anything.

Whisper.sh

Growing up with unhealthy personality traits was the start of my journey with BPD. They were coping mechanisms that worked for me as a young child. The older I got the less helpful they became and actually caused more problems than not. As a result I cannot regulate my emotions and there tend to be wild swings in my moods. BPD can often be misdiagnosed as bipolar disorder for this reason. I am all or nothing.

I feel out of control when my moods are extreme. I want someone to come in and lead me to wellness. I constantly feel an emptiness inside that may never fully go away. I need reassurance and acceptance constantly. It doesn't matter if nothing is wrong, I will still need you to keep reassuring me.

BPD is often linked to trauma at a young age and for me that was my inability to make relationships or even understand them. In my teenage years I desperately wanted to be accepted so I would cling to friendships so tightly I would drive the friends away. I would develop unhealthy obsessions with people and want to spend all my time with them. I lived in the pockets of my friend Dawn and her sister Stephanie so much when we were growing up that their brother used to hate seeing me coming. During my first real relationship with a boy, I used to love spending time at his house, especially with his mother, but his sister was nasty to me and kept telling me to go home. When these friends inevitably pulled away, it reinforced my feelings of abandonment and of not being good enough.

I've heard varied opinions on BPD over the last two years since my diagnosis. A lot of people think it's simply attention-seeking behaviour. I wish it were that easy. Most children as they grow and develop learn to self-soothe when they are upset and realise that what they're upset about isn't such a big deal. People who suffer with BPD, however, don't know how to soothe themselves or logically look at situations. So everything that upsets them appears to be a catastrophe. It's when we catastrophise that self-harm usually starts to appear. I know that when I got very upset it would often turn to anger, as I didn't know why I was feeling that way. The anger would build and build – often turning inwards – until I self-harmed to release that emotion. I believe had I been better educated on BPD I might have seen a pattern sooner.

I am convinced that, with earlier diagnoses, we can most definitely help sufferers get a better grasp on their condition.

With more education and conversation on this disorder, hopefully nobody else will have to go twenty years without a diagnosis.

A lot of behaviour patterns can be ignored in the teenage years and passed off as hormones raging or mood swings. In many cases it often is just teenage hormones, but it's when these patterns worsen or have no logic behind them that you need to sit down and wonder if it's something else. Is it a personality disorder? If so, how do you intervene?

I wrote earlier about how one of the hardest things to do is show someone with BPD that they are acting irrationally. For example, say you fall and cut your knee. Now you feel it bleeding, so no matter how many people might say that you are not bleeding, you will go with your own feelings. This is what it's like to have BPD. BPD sufferers feel that raw emotion – that wound – so strongly that we react, thinking our world is over, and we can't understand why others don't see it. As a BPD sufferer, every single emotion tears through my body, winding me.

Mental health issues can be as ruthless as cancer. They drive through society, uninterested in the carnage left behind.

I am medicated at the moment. I am also engaged in weekly psychology appointments and have completed extensive practices with a mental health nurse, social worker and occupational therapist. The important part of this story is I am not privileged; I am not paying for any special treatment. I see my mental health team as a public patient and have done so from the start. I would not be able to afford private treatment.

I know the HSE, especially in the last year, has gotten a lot of stick about mental health services in Ireland, but I have always said that I could never fault my services, as they have been top class from start to finish.

However, funding of our mental health services does have to change. I attended a Union of Students in Ireland and mental health reform rally outside Leinster House a few months ago. It was lashing rain, but Kildare Street was still packed and everyone was very angry. There were signs and placards being held by family members who'd lost loved ones, as well as people who, in despair, had made attempts on their own lives.

They were all there for one reason. They were sick of mental health taking the back seat with regards to funding and wanted a commitment to look at better funding for the future. Everyone was there for #IAmAReason. Conor Cusack, the brother of the former Cork hurler, Donal Óg Cusack, spoke like he was giving a speech at the 1916 Rising. The crowd cheered as he said what was on everyone's mind. It just isn't good enough any more. The entertainer Shane Gillen spoke about his brother-in-law, gone because of inadequate mental health intervention. I also spoke at the rally. As someone who isn't cured but who is living with a mental health illness, I believed that my voice might help those who were too ashamed to stand up and be counted, and also support those who stood before me in the lashing rain.

52

BUILDING YOUR EMOTIONAL SUPPORT

People must know that recovery is possible.
We need to move from maintenance to recovery.

www.mentalhealthreform.ie

In hindsight, it may sound odd to you, but I am so glad that I had the mental breakdown in August 2015. It was, of course, awful that it had to happen, and when it did a part of me died – the erratic, spontaneous me. I found it hard not to have that part of me any more, I felt it put me on the back foot, made me less adequate. But without the breakdown I would still be walking against the wind, unable to comprehend what my emotions were trying to tell me. Now I have been diagnosed and am being treated by a multidisciplinary team who are making a real difference. It's not just about the medication – all aspects of the treatment are just as important as each other.

I understand that BPD is part of who I am and although I will try to stay ahead of it I am sure, at times, it will get the better of me. I still live with the fear of abandonment. I live with horrific body image issues that I will have to work through in therapy. In fact, my body image – or lack of one – is at the core of a lot of my worries. I still spend so much time chastising myself and self-loathing that I mentally exhaust myself to the point where self-harming can seem like the only answer.

But I am getting better. I haven't self-harmed in a while. I did harm myself a few months ago in sheer emotional distress, but I stopped before it spiralled out of control. Because of the medication I have the luxury of a delay now – time to collect my thoughts before I act. It is making life a lot easier for those close to me because I can express myself in a healthier and more productive way.

A lot of people feel that they are only getting to know me now, as I was so hot and cold before. I find people aren't as afraid to approach me. I was so defensive before, as I had this very solid wall built around me.

My family relationships will be harder to repair. Keeping interpersonal relationships healthy and functioning is one of the hardest things to do when battling BPD. Emotional dysregulation makes mood swings become mood rollercoasters. There's a lifetime of confusion there that I'm only beginning to work through now. One of my biggest regrets is missing out on some of my nieces' and nephews' lives because I was too emotionally unpredictable to be relied on.

My worst nightmare has always been losing Frank. He is my one, I truly believe that. But writing this memoir brought up difficult memories and experiences and caused me to slip into past patterns of pretending everything was okay, hiding bills in drawers, pretending I was feeling better, while missing my medication. Starving myself, then bingeing. And I'm extremely sad to say that I finally managed to push him away. After six years together and two years of marriage, we separated.

I am still very much in love with Frank and always will be to a certain level. He gave me a glimpse that fairytales may exist but I'm not there yet. He gave me Farah, the light of my life and my beacon of hope, and for that I will always be grateful.

I still have a lot to figure out about how to function healthily in life. After the separation I fell into a period of denial, hoping he'd stay with me. Hating him one minute and pleading with him the next – *I hate you, please don't leave me*. Thankfully I have managed to move past this and we remain friends. We are working to ensure that we have the best relationship we can so that we can give Farah the life she deserves. We are good parents and we will stay good friends – I absolutely believe that.

I won't allow myself to become immersed in the pain of losing him, because if I do I will only fall back into the patterns of destructive behaviour that my BPD causes. And going back is not what I do – only moving forward. I have to learn to accept that I will likely never love who I am, but that it's okay to let others love me. That's an uncomfortable feeling that I'm learning to live with. For me, constantly trying to fix the past stunted my ability to live. Now I live for today, for here and now. What will be, will be.

Someone who suffers with BPD
isn't locked up with the key thrown away,
it's not a spoilt child kicking the wall –
it's me,
I'm BPD.

Nikki Hayes

NOT THE END

ACKNOWLEDGEMENTS

Firstly I want to thank my husband Frank for his patience and love, and for making me see that happiness is possible. I will never be able to express my gratitude to him for giving me Farah. She is the child I never thought I'd have and she has exceeded every dream I may have had in having a daughter. She is stunningly beautiful, mischievous, loving and intelligent. Frank extended his limits time and time again to try to keep me in his future but I want him to know that I understand that BPD won this time. It's extremely upsetting and difficult to live with someone with BPD but he managed it for a long time. I will always love him and am heartbroken we couldn't make it work.

Farah, my angel, my reason to live. You make me smile. You fill my life with real love and hope. I will continue to fight so you never have to. You are perfectly you – I'll make sure you always see that. I look forward to seeing you become everything you want to be.

Dad – ten years on and a piece of me left with you. I miss you every day.

Dessie and Mary Black, my in-laws for a time and forever my family. I love you both and will never be able to thank you enough for your love and unconditional support. Thank you from the bottom of my heart for everything. A gentleman and lady always.

Audrey, thank you for your continuous support. You've been by my side always, helping me into a taxi after too hard a night, drying my tears over the years and sitting by my bed when I was frightened and locked away in hospital. Paul, you have been there to help me fill in the blanks and supported me no matter what. You both are friends that I wouldn't be here without.

Claire, my sista sista, you came into my life through Farah – if that wasn't a sign from above I don't know what is. I firmly believe you were sent to me.

Conor, you were my lifeline when I hid in isolation, you were my only friend at a time when you didn't even know it. Farah is as blessed to have you as her godfather as I am to call you a friend.

Dev, Trolley, Thelma – long-term friends, you still make me laugh. Kelly, Lyndsay – salt of the earth.

Sinead Desmond, Melanie Finn, Laura Butler and Irish media, thank you for always carrying my story with such care and compassion.

Louis Walsh, Joanne Byrne and Sinead Ryan – you raised me up at a time when all I wanted to do was fall.

Markus Feehily, thank you for your voice which has helped me push through some very difficult times.

Jean, Pauline, Orla, Vera, Sean and all at Abbeytots Crèche, you have become so much more than Farah's childcare – you have become friends.

Martina, thank you for always being there with a sympathetic ear and a cup of coffee, your friendship means the world to me. Siobhan, you warrior.

Annie and Ashley Staunton, thank you for holding my hand when I didn't even want to hold on, I'll never forget that.

My nieces and nephews, who I miss every day – there is always a way. Undiagnosed BPD led to family relationships lost and strained, but I will never give up hope.

And finally to every mental health advocate out there, you have given me the strength and support to tell my story by telling me yours. We are #strongertogether.

USEFUL CONTACTS

If you are affected by any of the topics covered in this book, remember you are not alone. There is help and you are worth it. You are a reason.

Pieta House
1800 247 247
www.pieta.ie

The Samaritans
1850 609 090
www.samaritans.org

Teenline Ireland
1800 833 634
www.teenline.ie

3Ts
01 2139905
www.3ts.ie

Bodywhys
1890 200 444
www.bodywhys.ie

In an emergency
112/999